CATS AND GEISHAS

COLORING BOOK

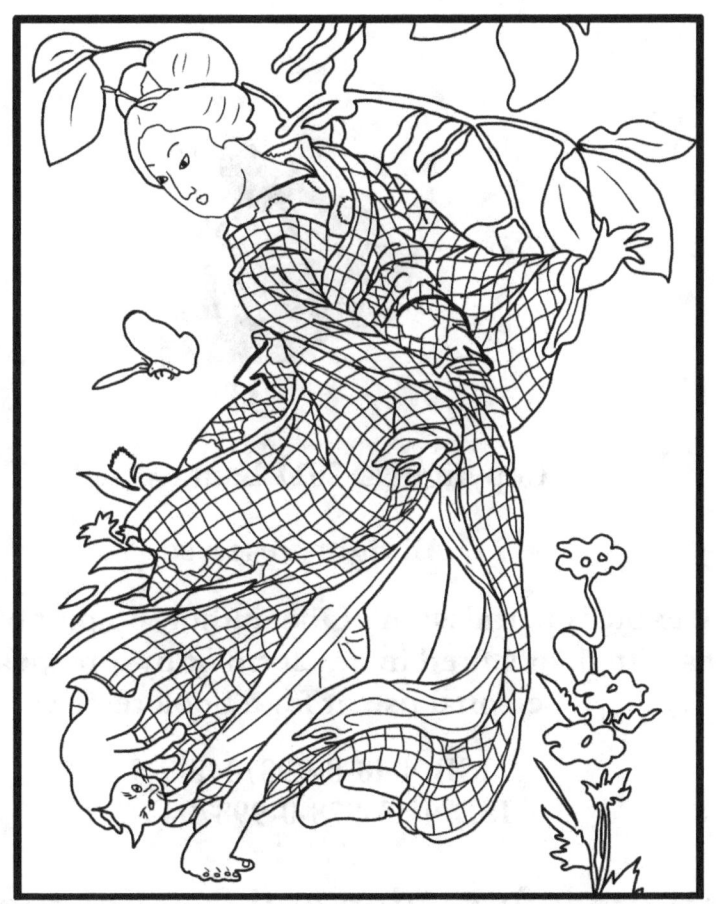

A Great Cat Publication

by

L.A. Vocelle

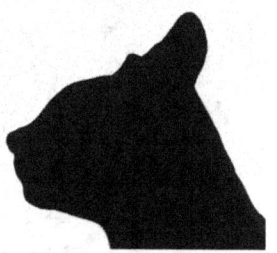

ISBN-10-0-9987042-2-9
ISBN-13-978-0-9987042-2-7

For more information and free downloads, visit
www.thegreatcat.org

DEDICATION

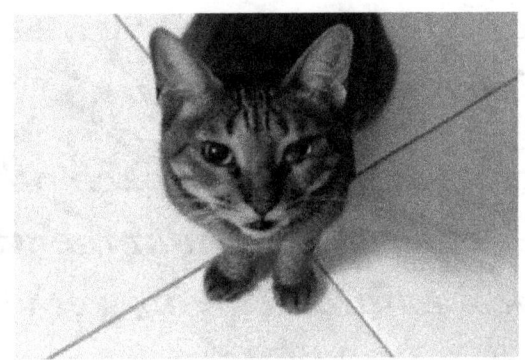

This book is dedicated to my little love, Beseechy Runtus.
We will meet again.

Dear Cat and Art Coloring Lovers,

This coloring book will provide you with hours of stress relieving relaxation while coloring historically based Ukiyo-e woodprints. Each coloring page shows a beautiful geisha interacting with a cat(s) and/or kitten(s).

The coloring pages in this book are based on public domain representations of Japanese Ukiyo-e art prints from the period (1603-1868). Translated, Ukiyo-e means a fleeting, transient world based on the Buddhist philosophy of impermanence. Ukiyo-e works were mostly woodblock prints, and the primary subjects were landscapes, seascapes, geishas and cats, colored with vegetable dyes and then copied for mass consumption. This new art form was supported by the newly wealthy merchant class who were expressly interested in pleasure.

Geishas and cats were likened to each other just as women and cats have been equated throughout the world and history. Cats' enigmatic mystical nature of loving yet vicious, peaceful yet aggressive was also used to describe women. Therefore, cats were the perfect companions of geishas.

Some supernatural representations include demon cats (bakeneko) along with a geisha. These are based on folktales where geishas and courtesans were able to change into cats. Demon cats are easily spotted with a towel or napkin over their heads or sometimes with a forked tail.

The geishas and cats are portrayed in domestic scenes. Geishas are wearing colorful and intricately designed kimonos and are reading, writing, gardening or playing music, all attributes that a geisha must possess. Some cats are on leashes, and some are playing or humorously causing chaos.

For free downloadable coloring pages and other publications related to cats, visit The Great Cat website at www.thegreatcat.org. Subscribe to receive weekly updates on cats in art, history and literature. Find me on Facebook and join the group Coloring Books for Cat Lovers.

Let me hear from you! I'm always open to suggestions and improvements, so I welcome your emails: LAVocelle@thegreatcat.org.

If you purchased through Amazon, please leave a review.

Happy Coloring!

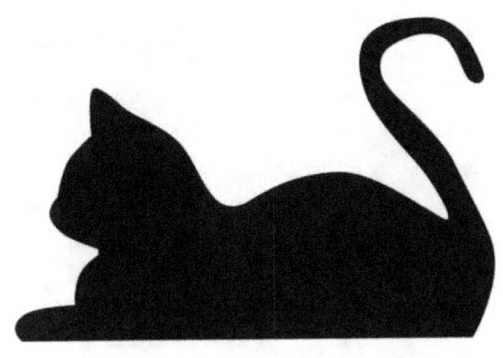

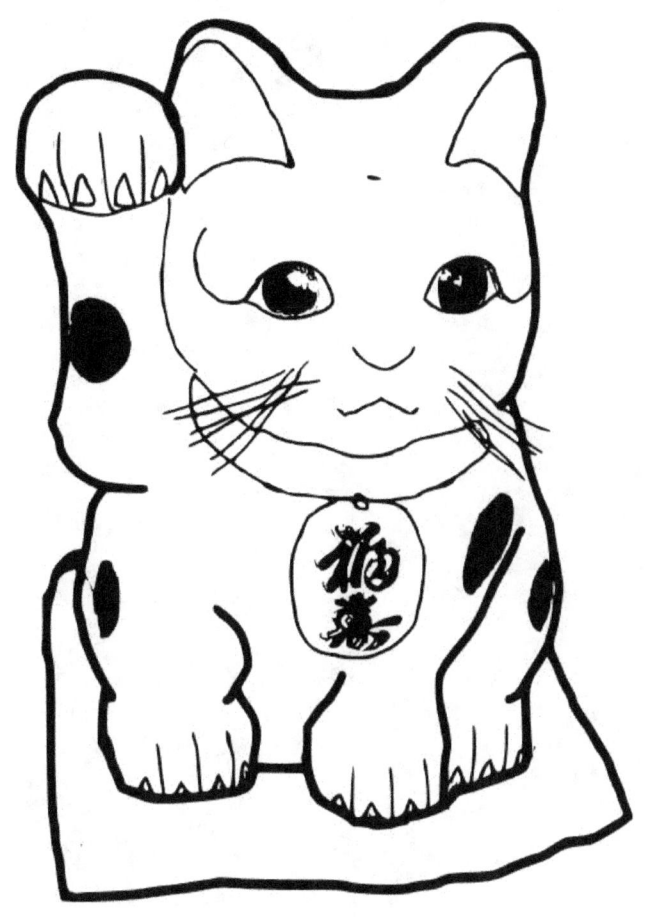

COLORED BY _____

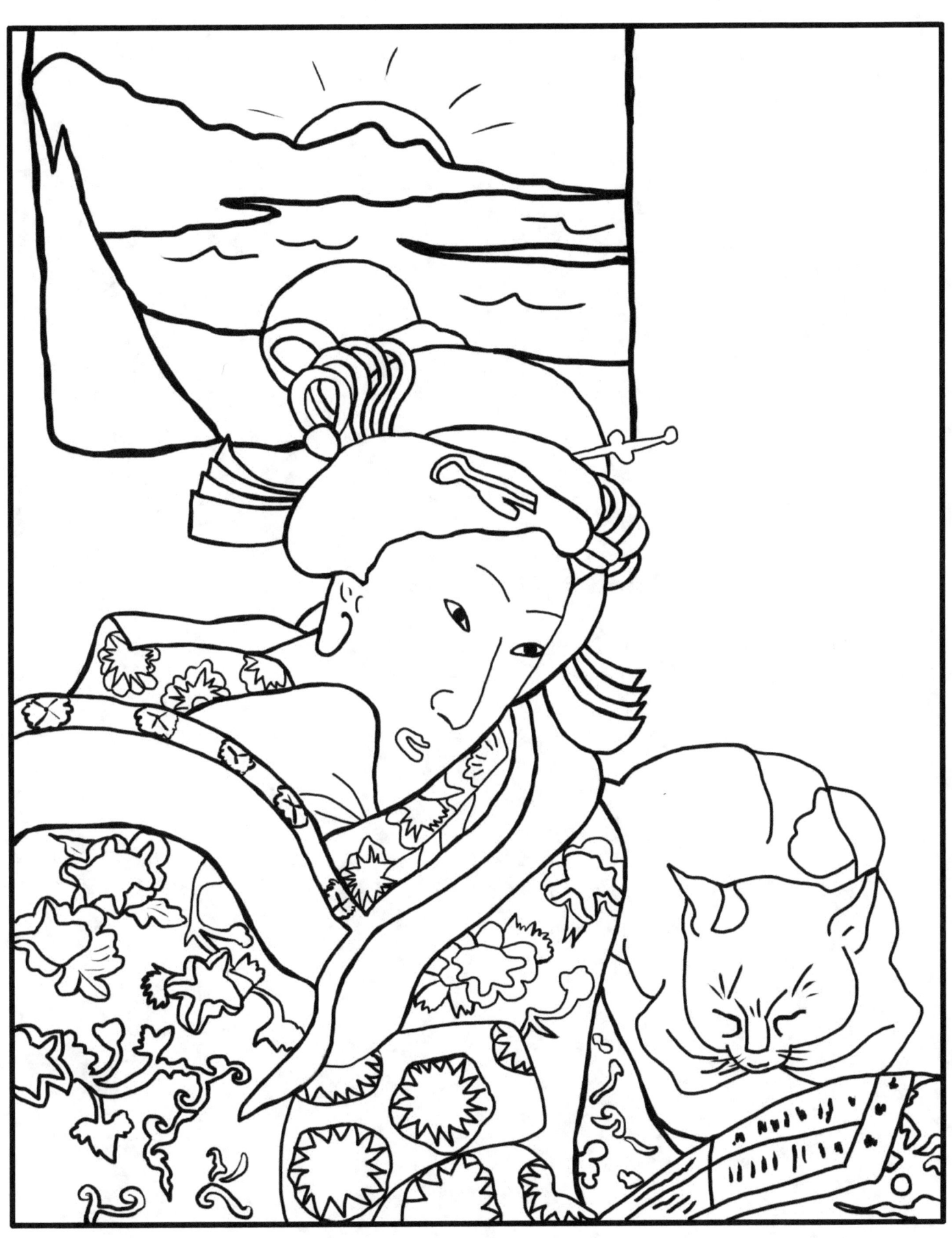

Woman Reading the Paper with her Cat, Utagawa Kuniyoshi, ca. 1800

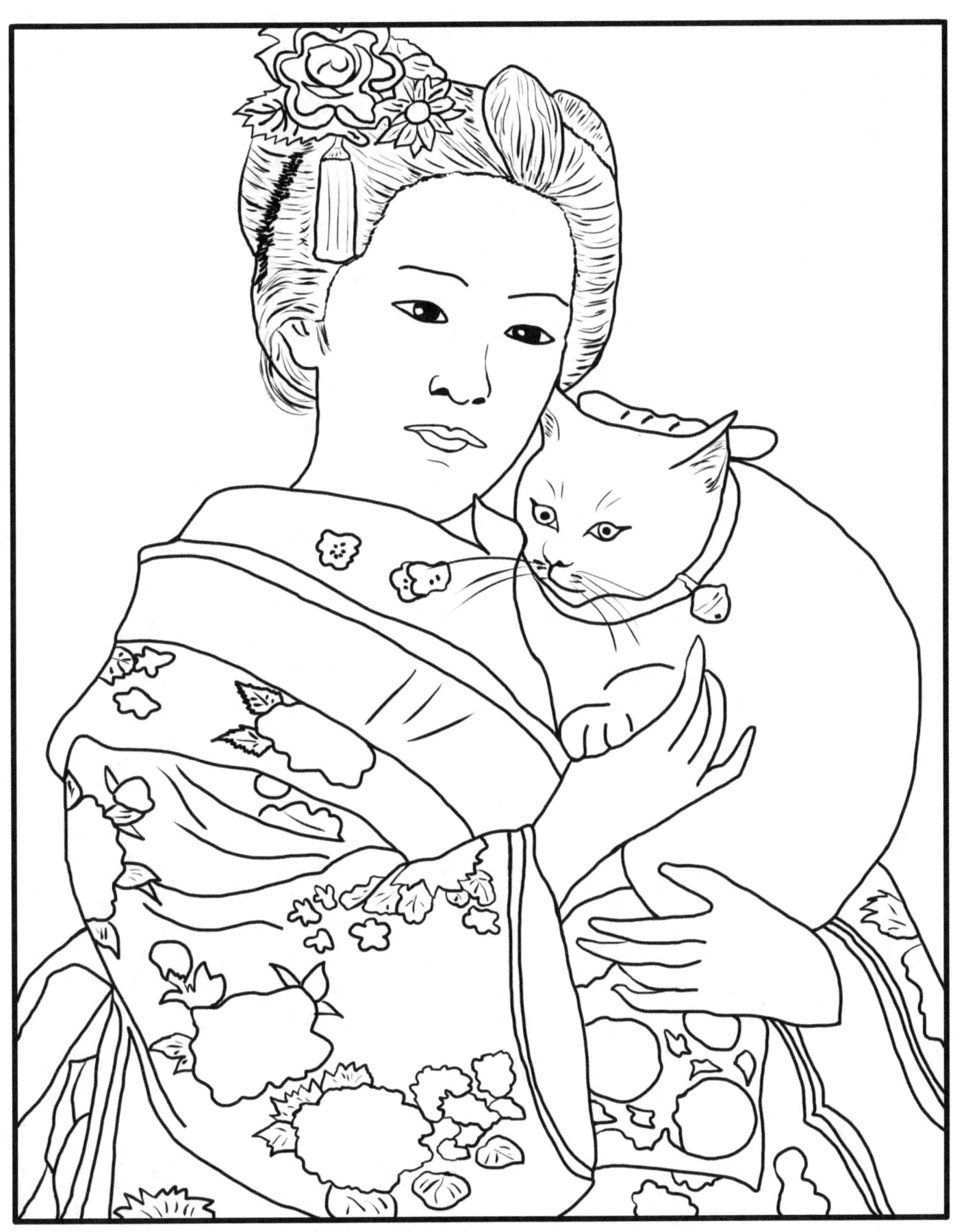

Geigi Koiku and her Cat, Anon, 1883

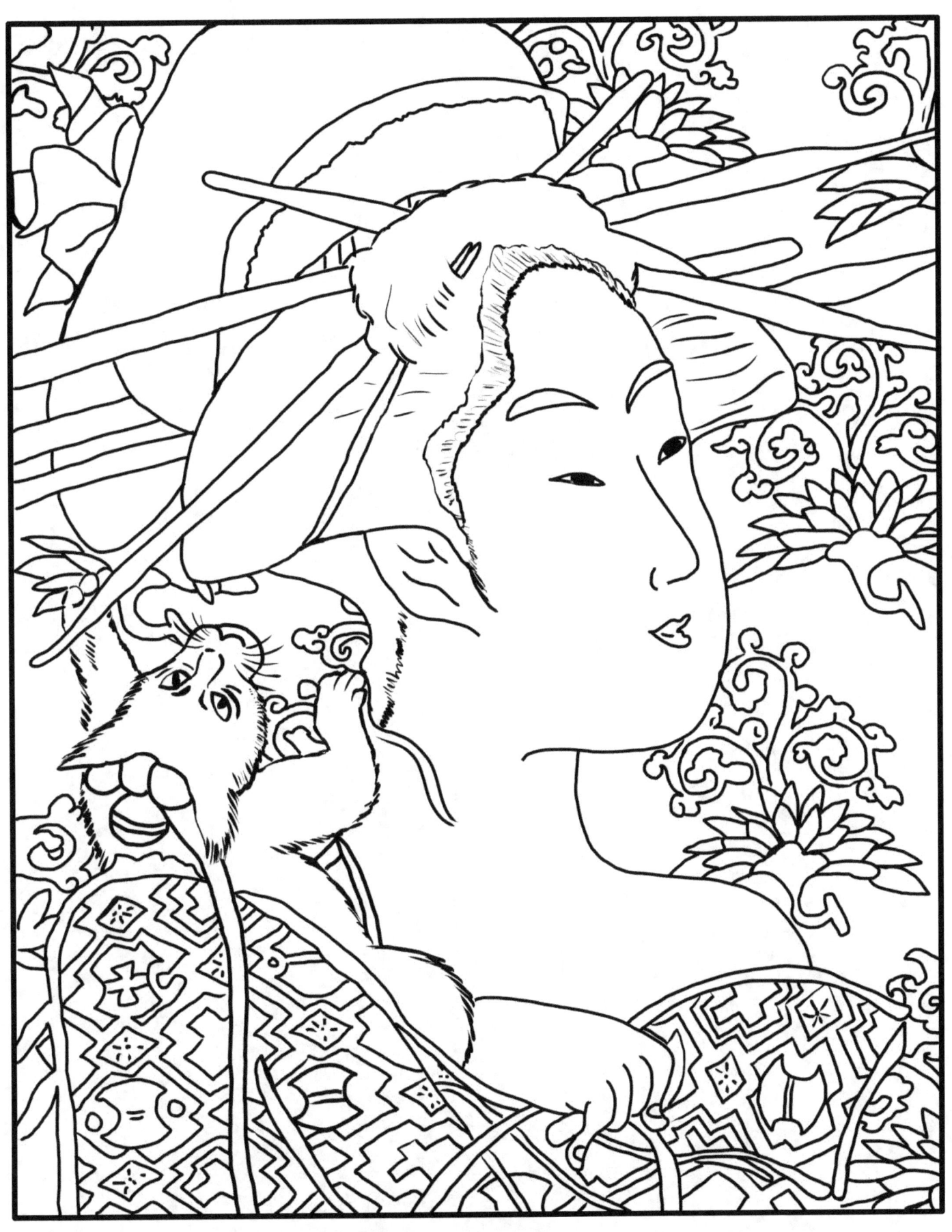

Cat Playing with a Geisha's Hair, Chokosai Eisho, 1795-97

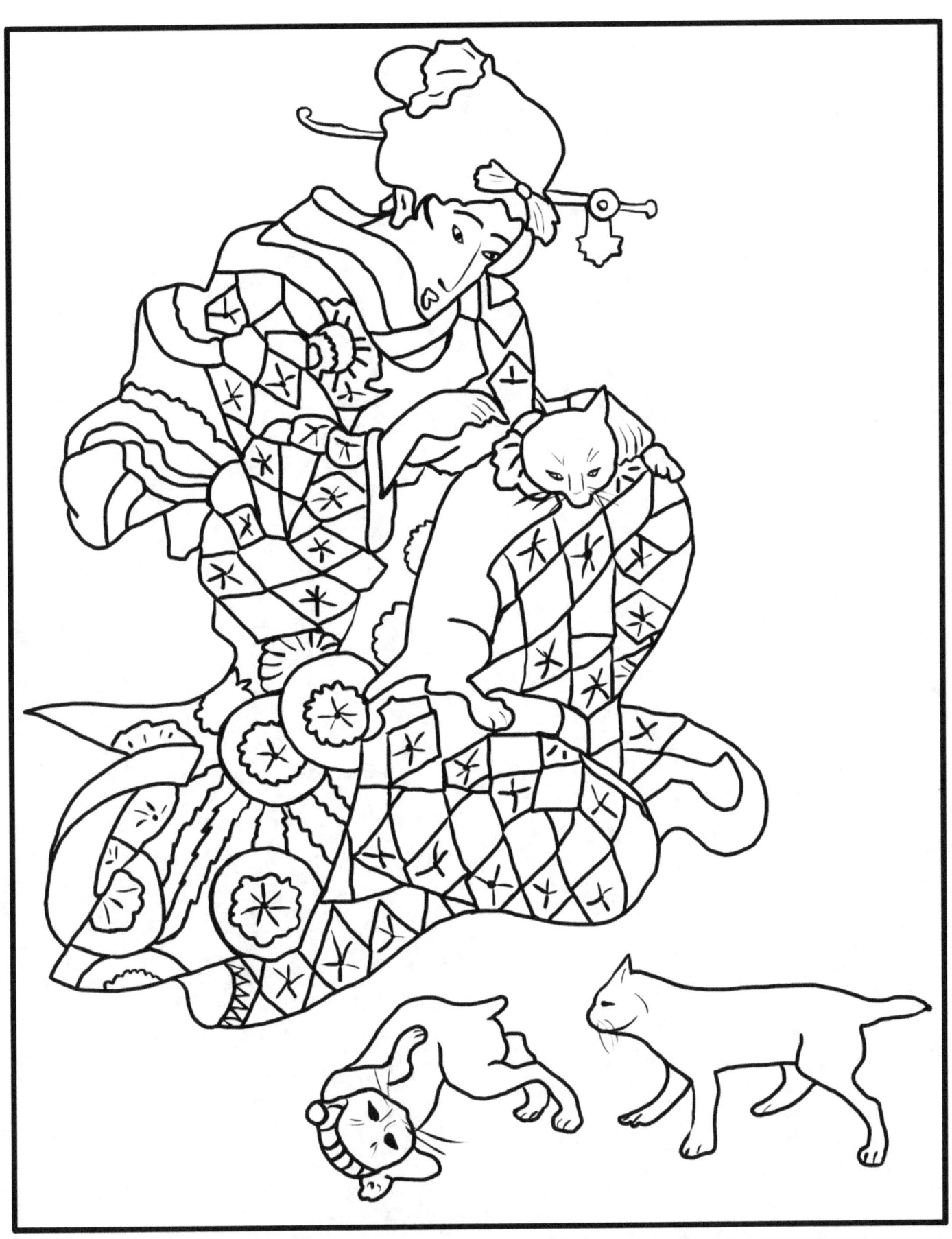

Beauty with Cats, Utagawa Kuniyoshi, ca. 1843

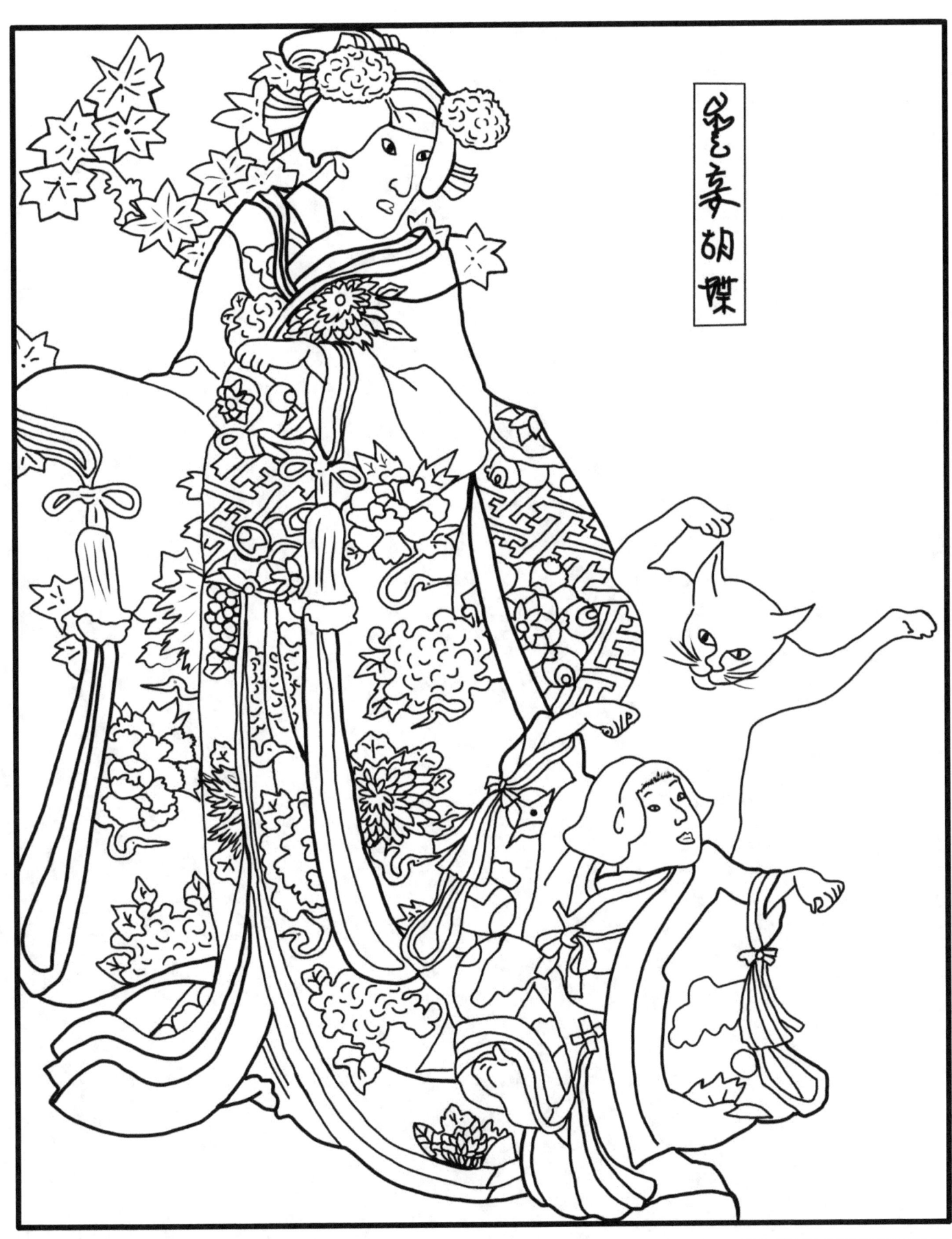

雪妾胡蝶

Dancing Cat and Child, Toyokuni Kunisada (1786 - 1860)

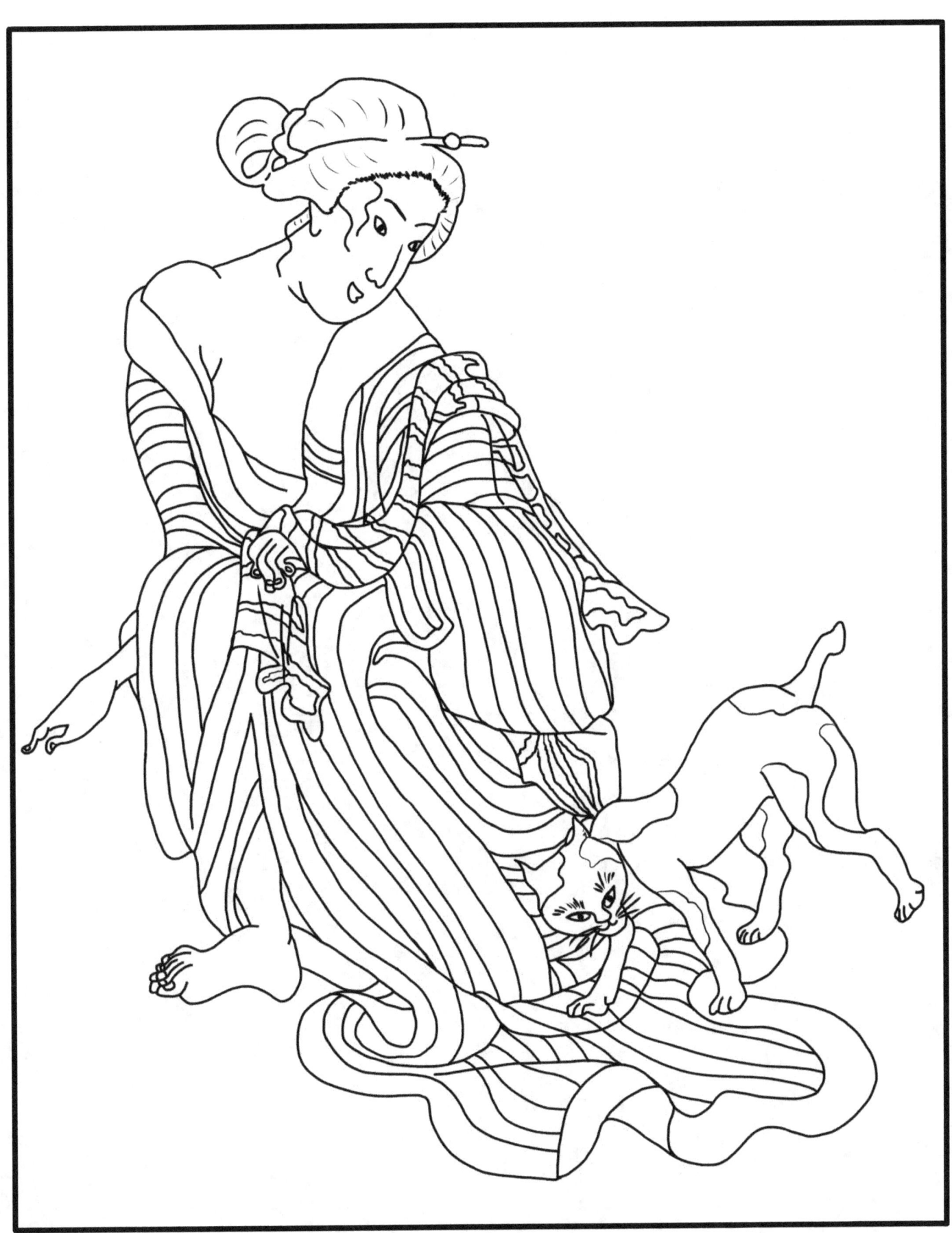

GEISHA AND CAT, UTAGAWA KONIYOSHI

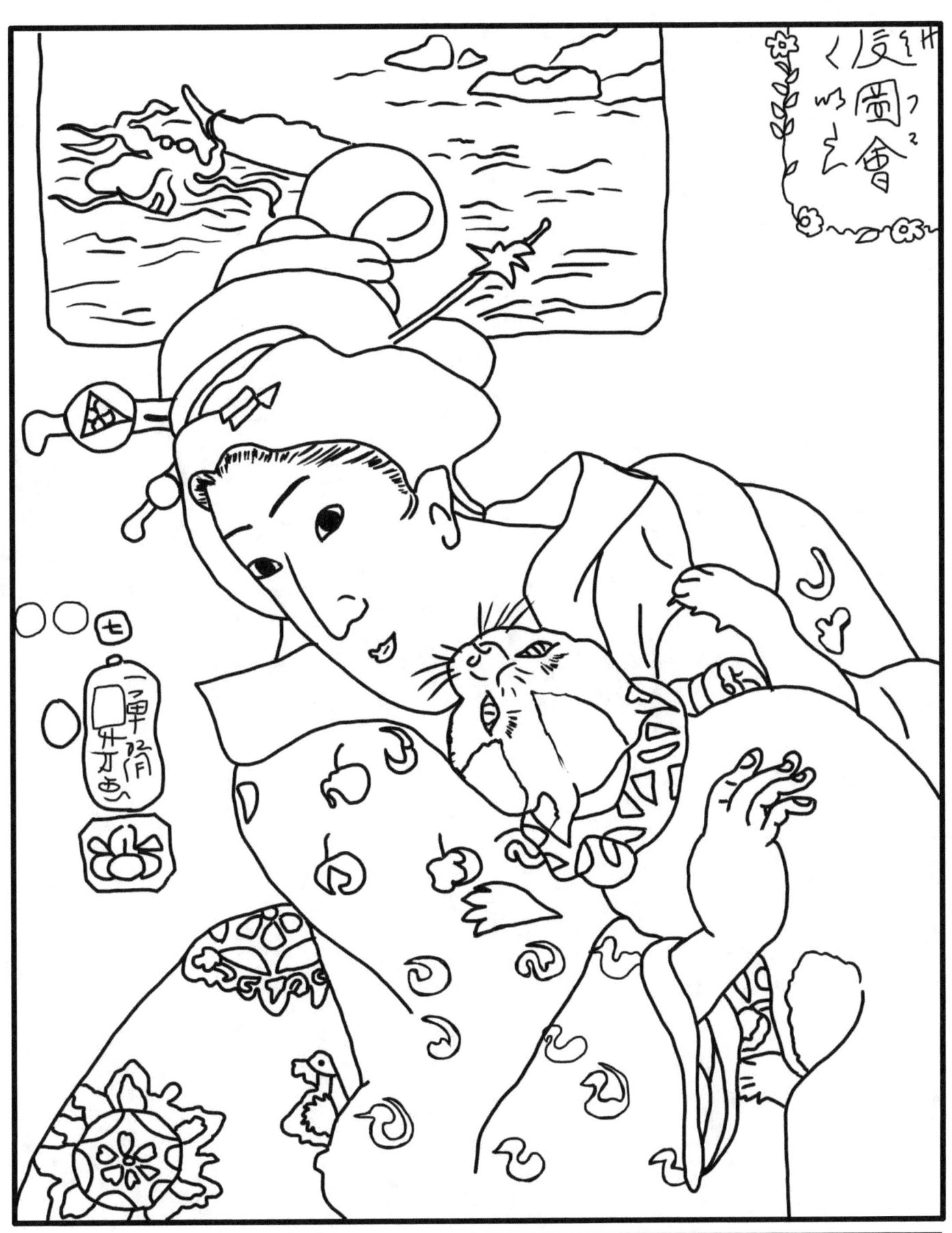

Geisha Holding a Cat, Utagawa Kuniyoshi

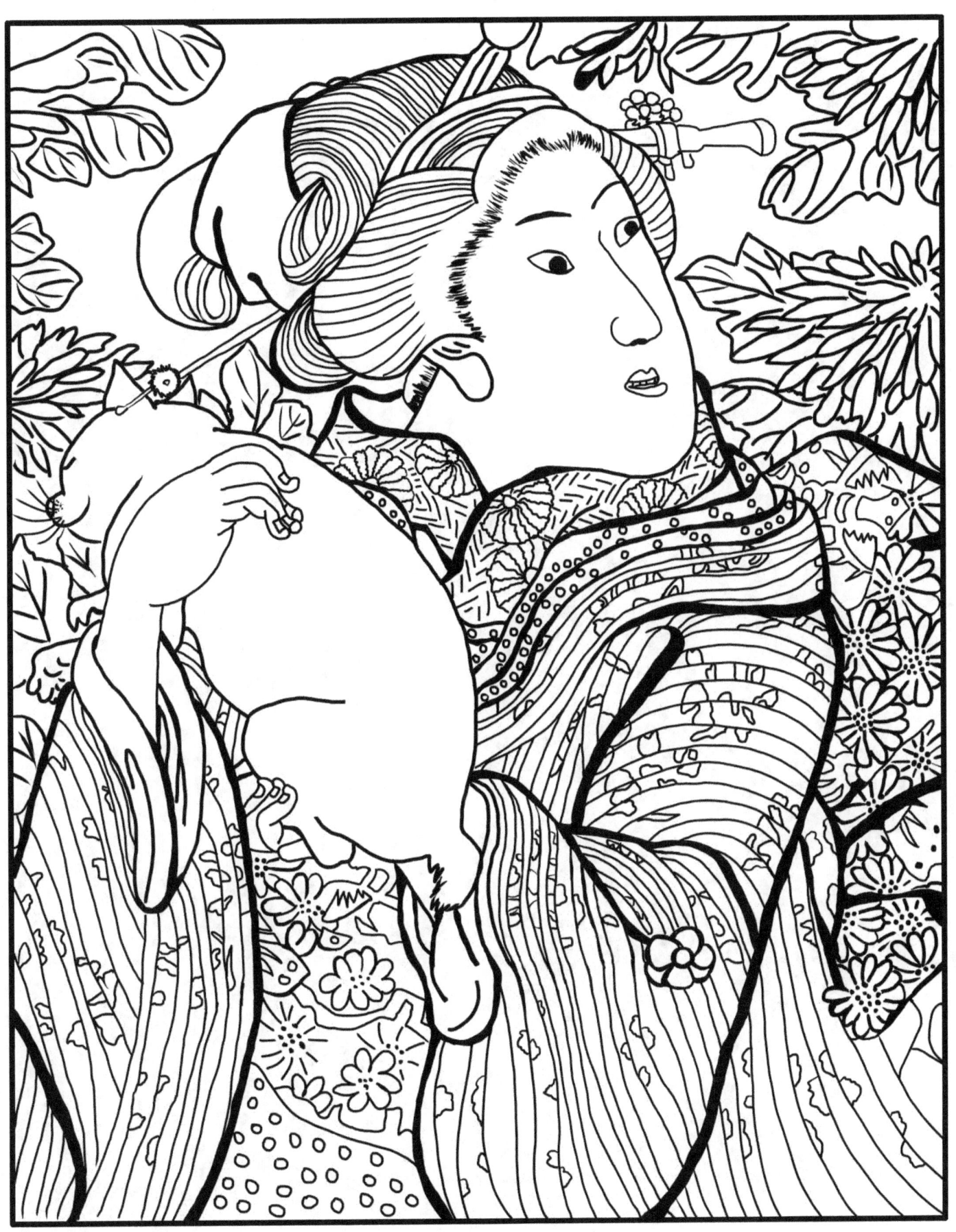

Chrysanthemums, Utagawa Kuniyoshi

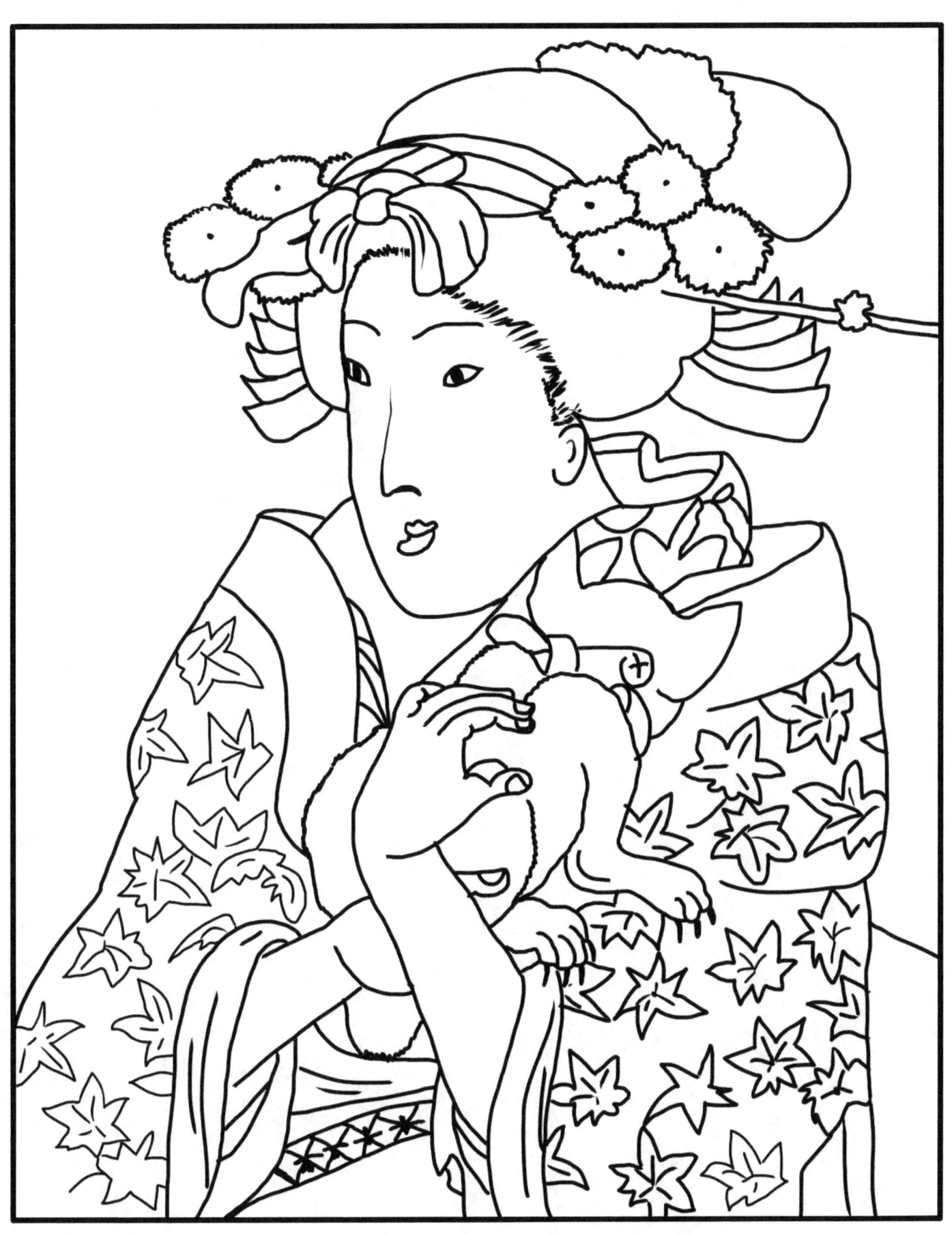

Beauty Holding a Cat, Eisen Ikeda, ca. 1843-1846

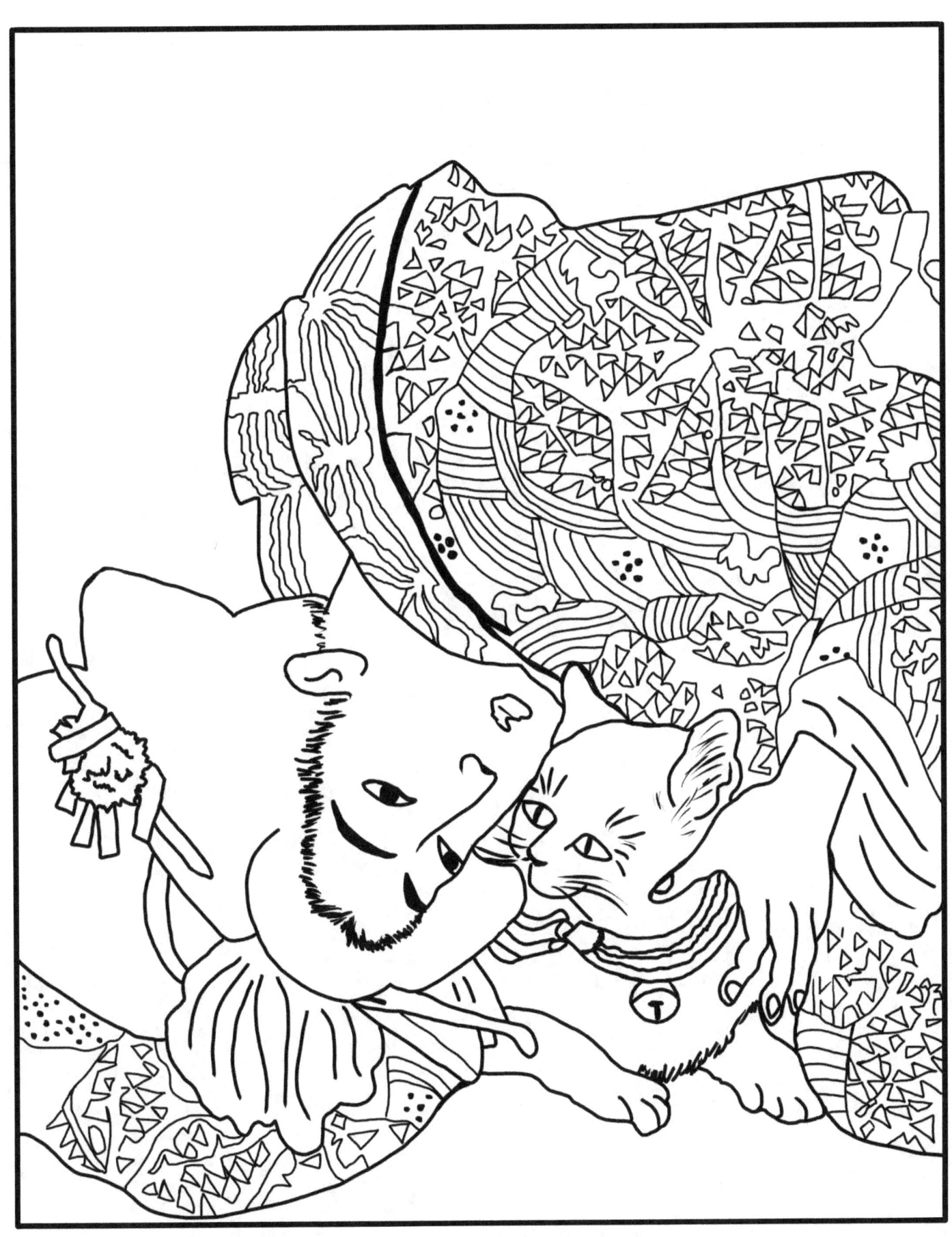

Geisha Embracing a Cat, Tsukioka Yoshitoshi

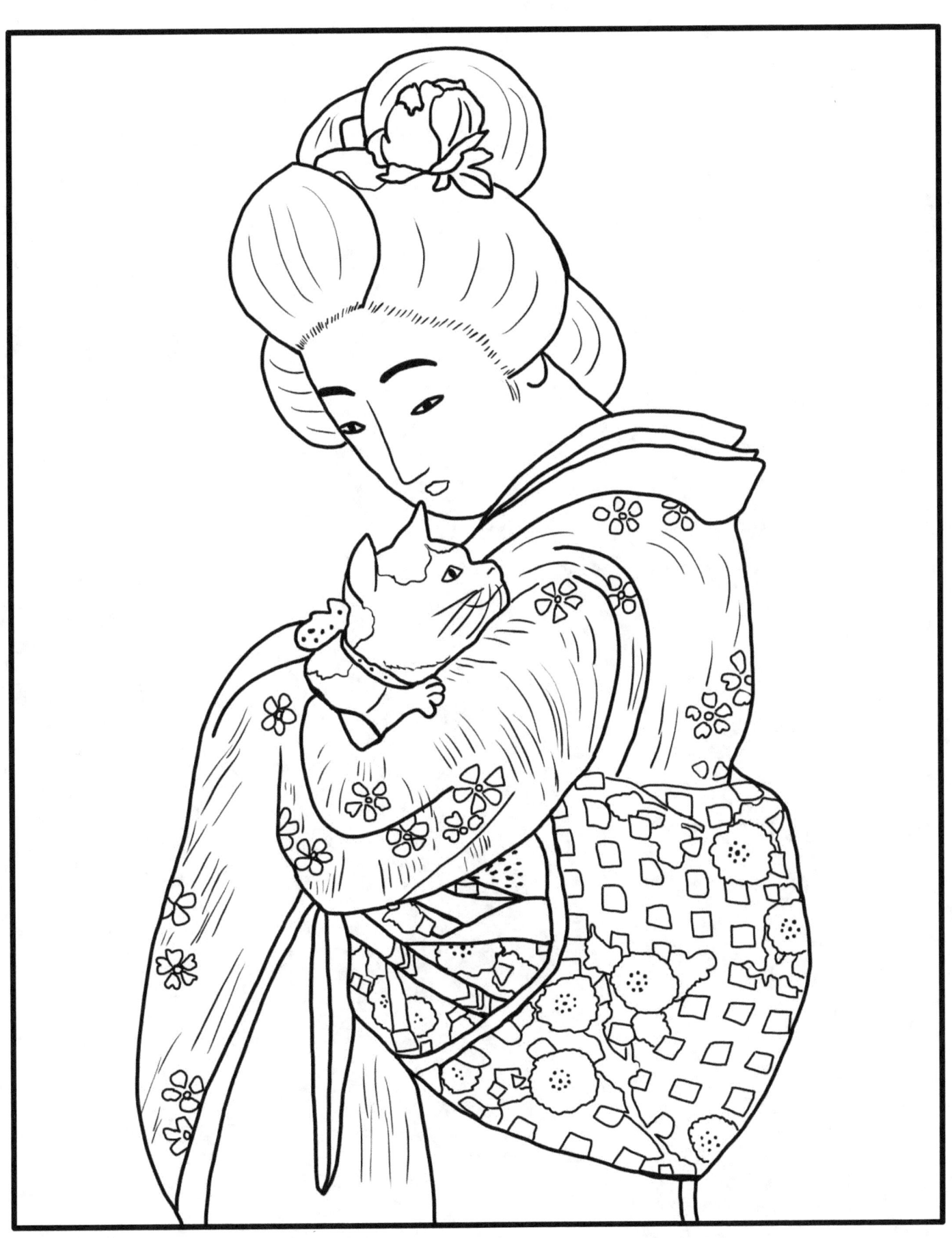

THE MERCHANT'S DAUGHTER, MIZUNO TOSHIKATA, 1900

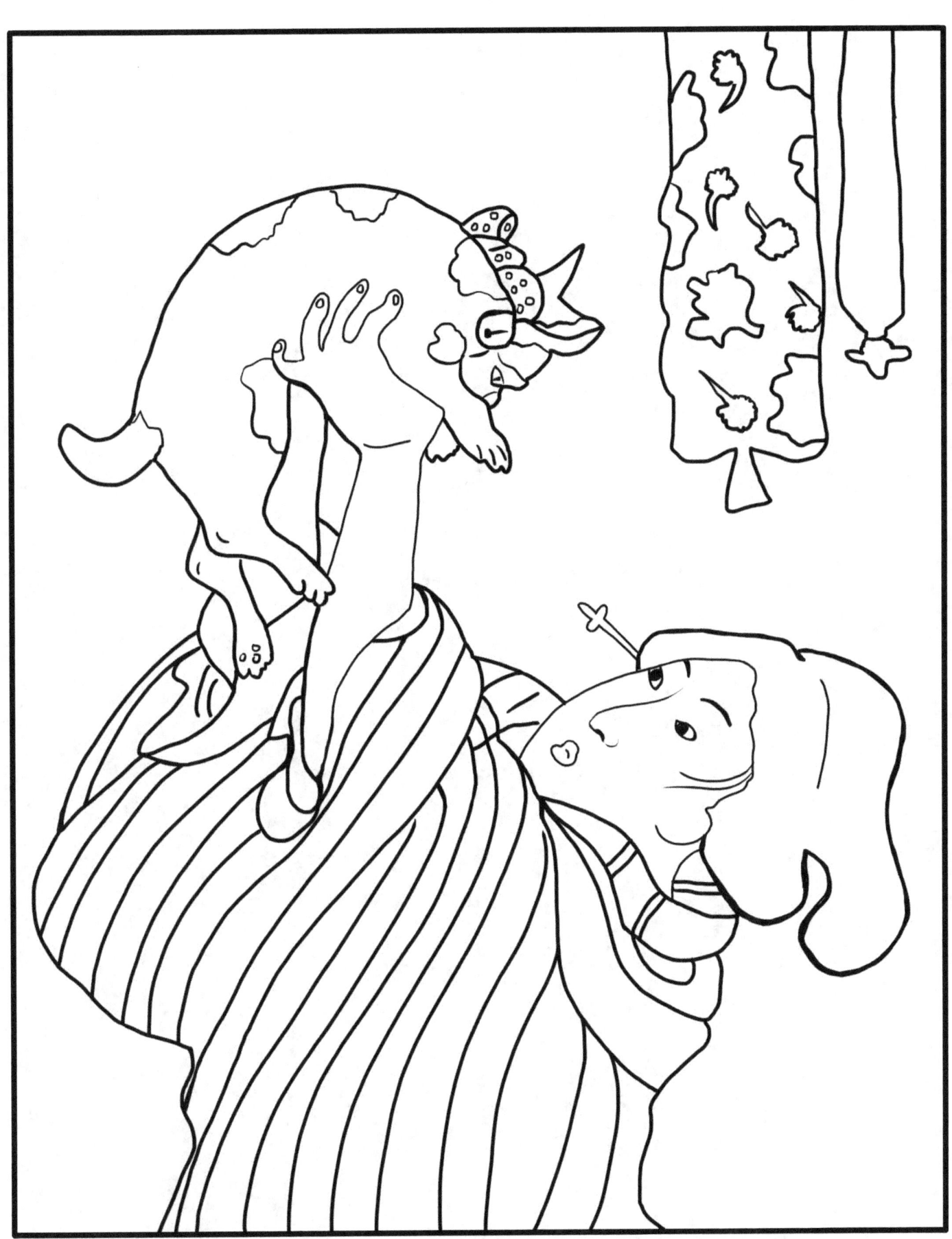

Geisha Holding a Cat, Toyohara Kunichika, 1835-1900

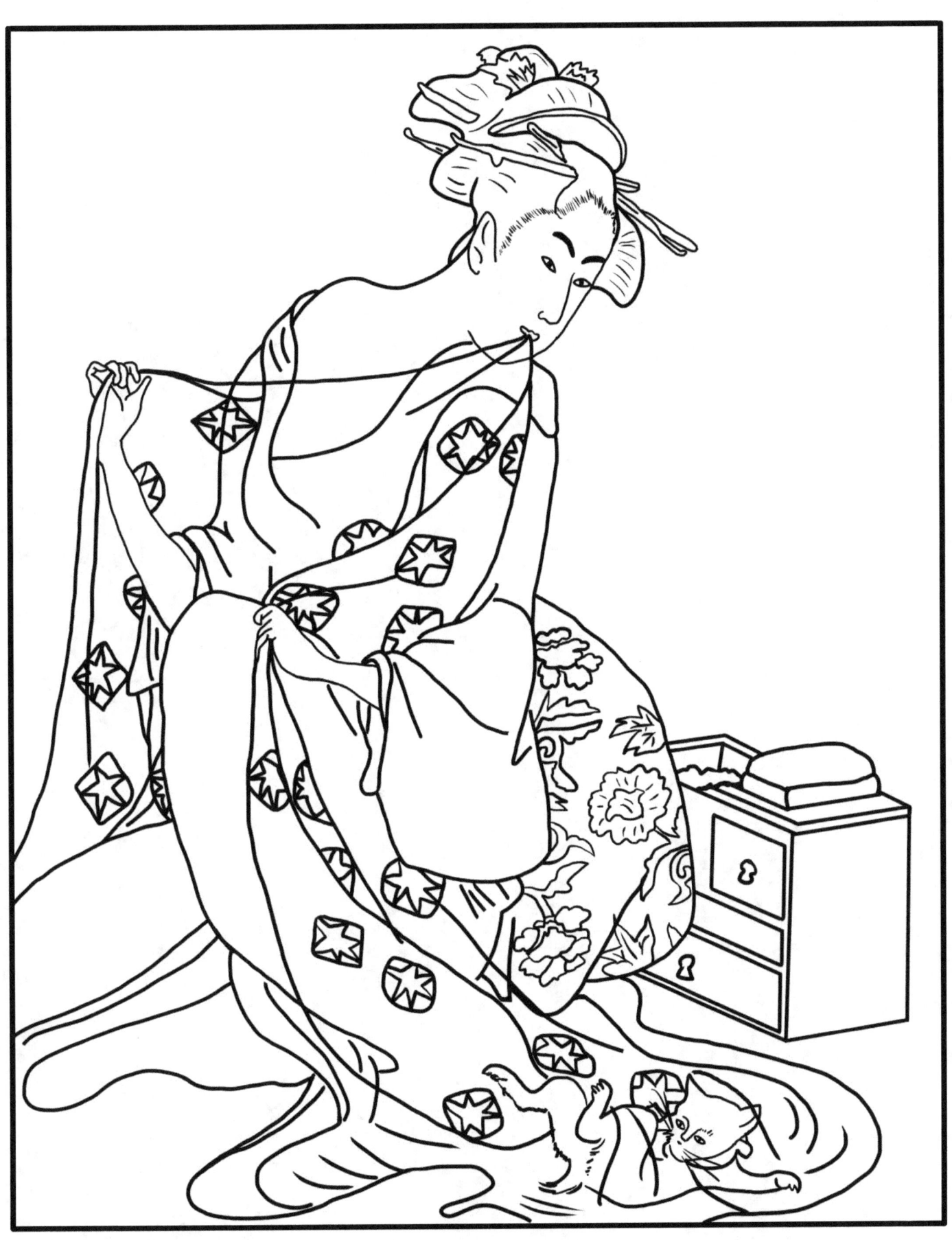

A Woman and a Playful Cat, Kitagawa Utamaro, 1793-94

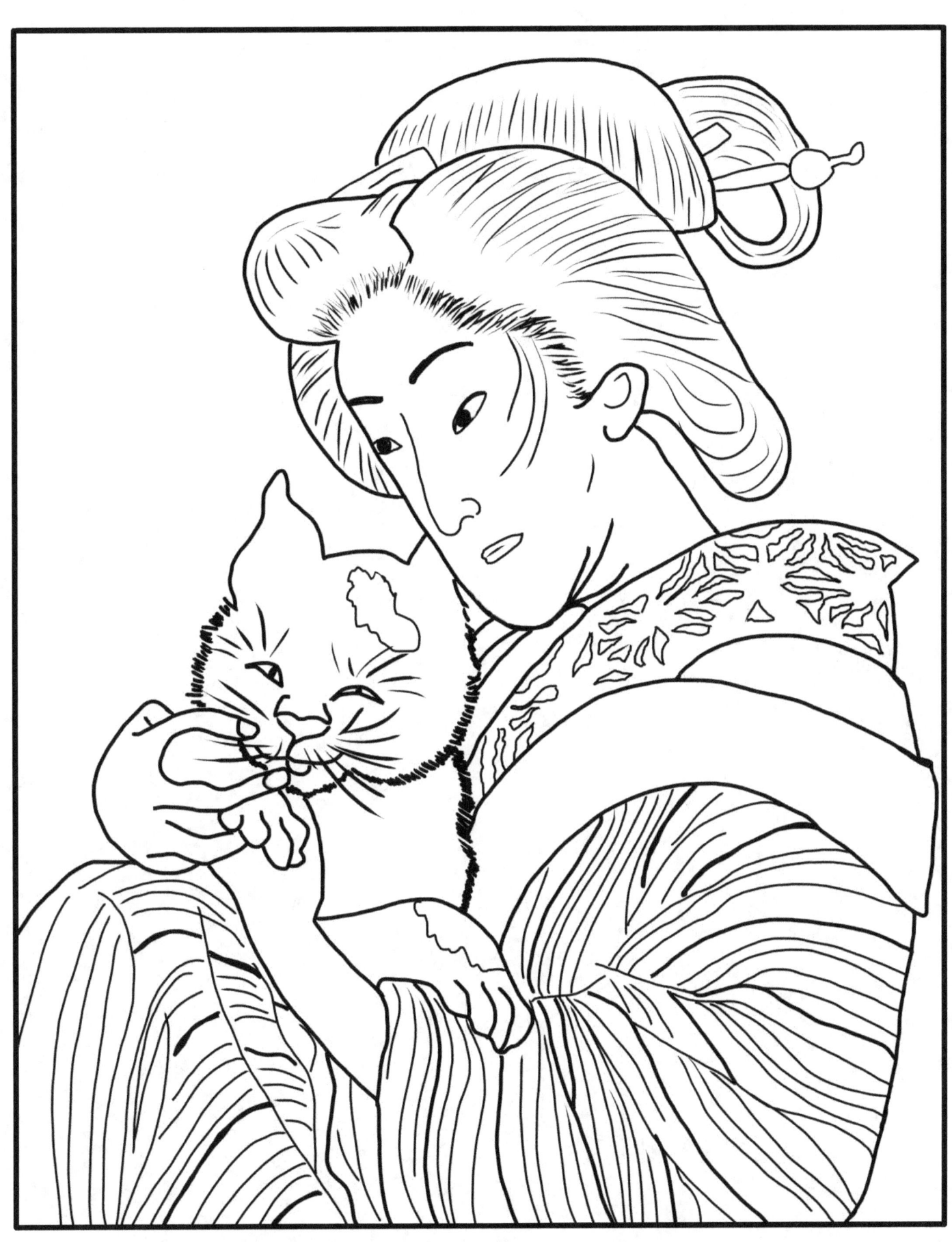

BIJUTSU SEKAI, TSUKIOKA YOSHITOSHI, 1890

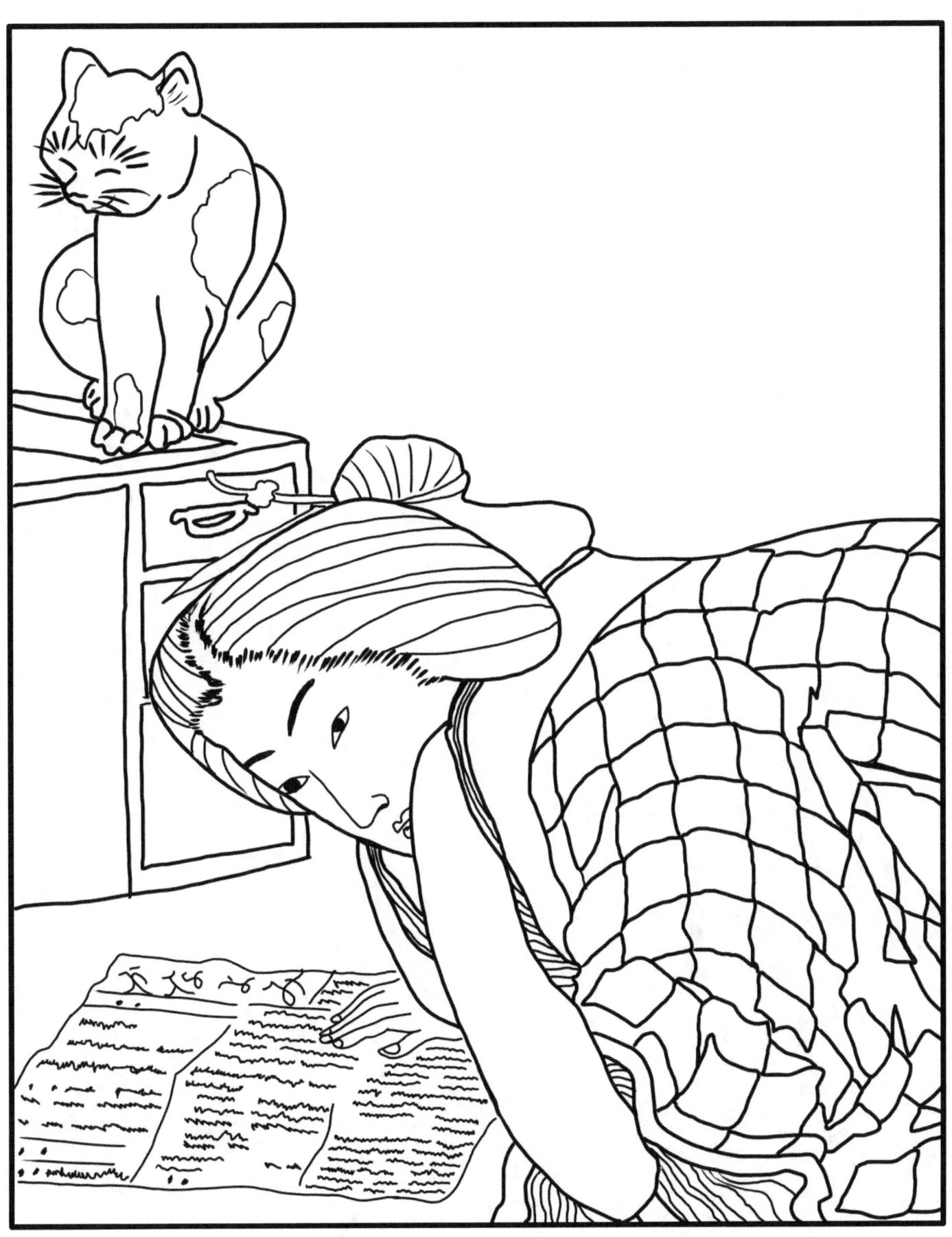

Woman Reading with her Cat, Tsukioka Yoshitoshi

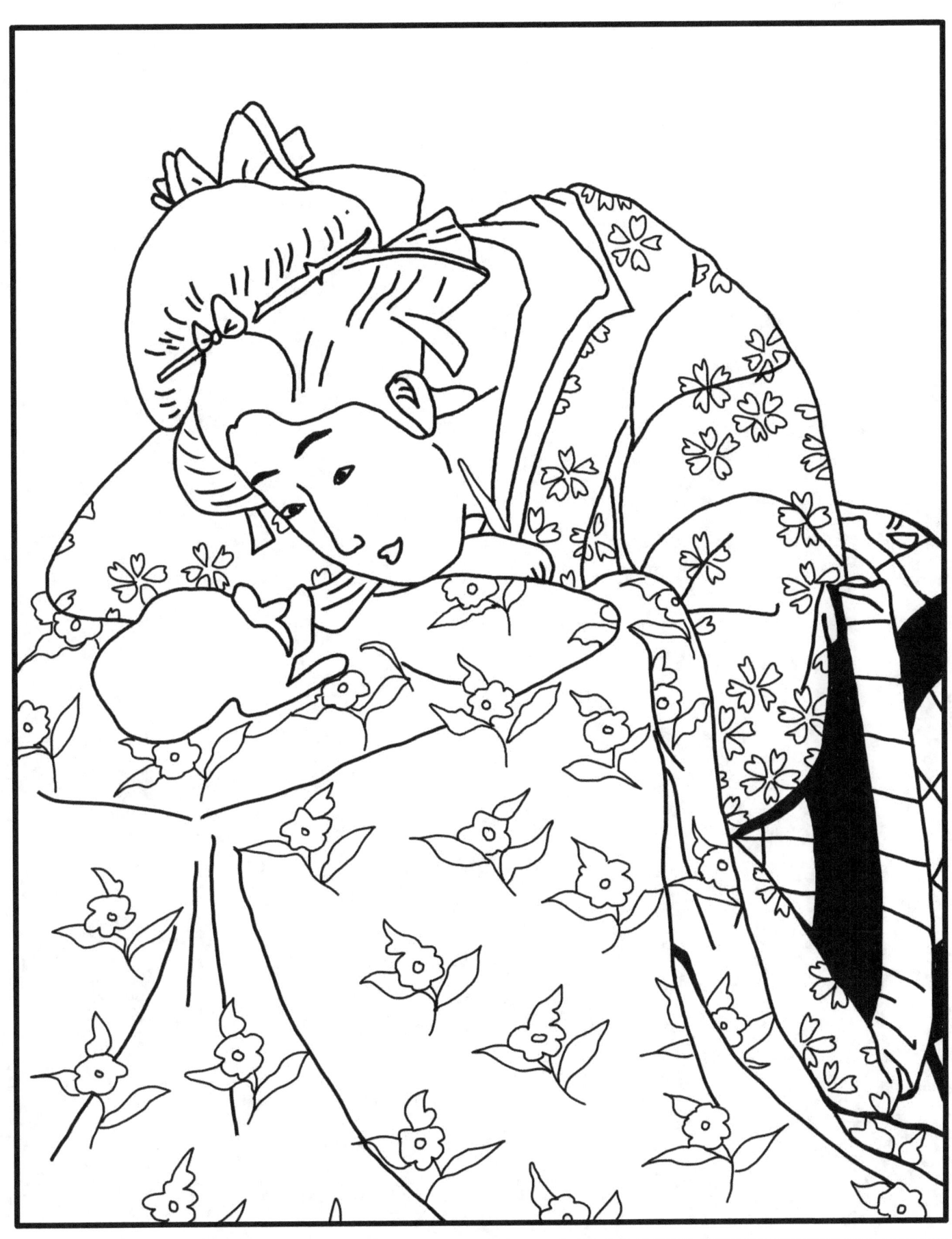

Woman and Cat, Kotatsu de Asobu Onna, 1796

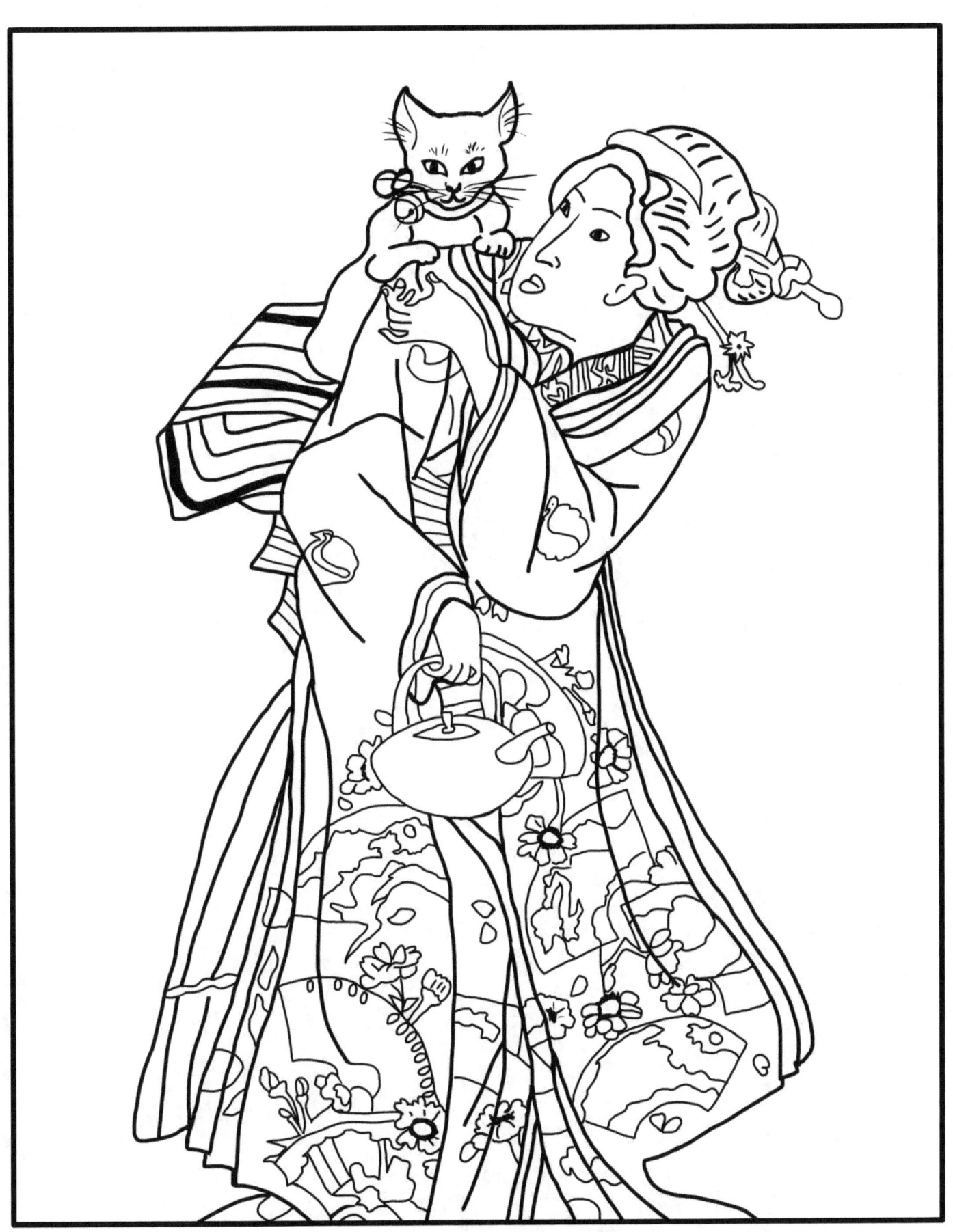

GEISHA WITH CAT ON HER SHOULDER, UTAGAWA KUNISADA

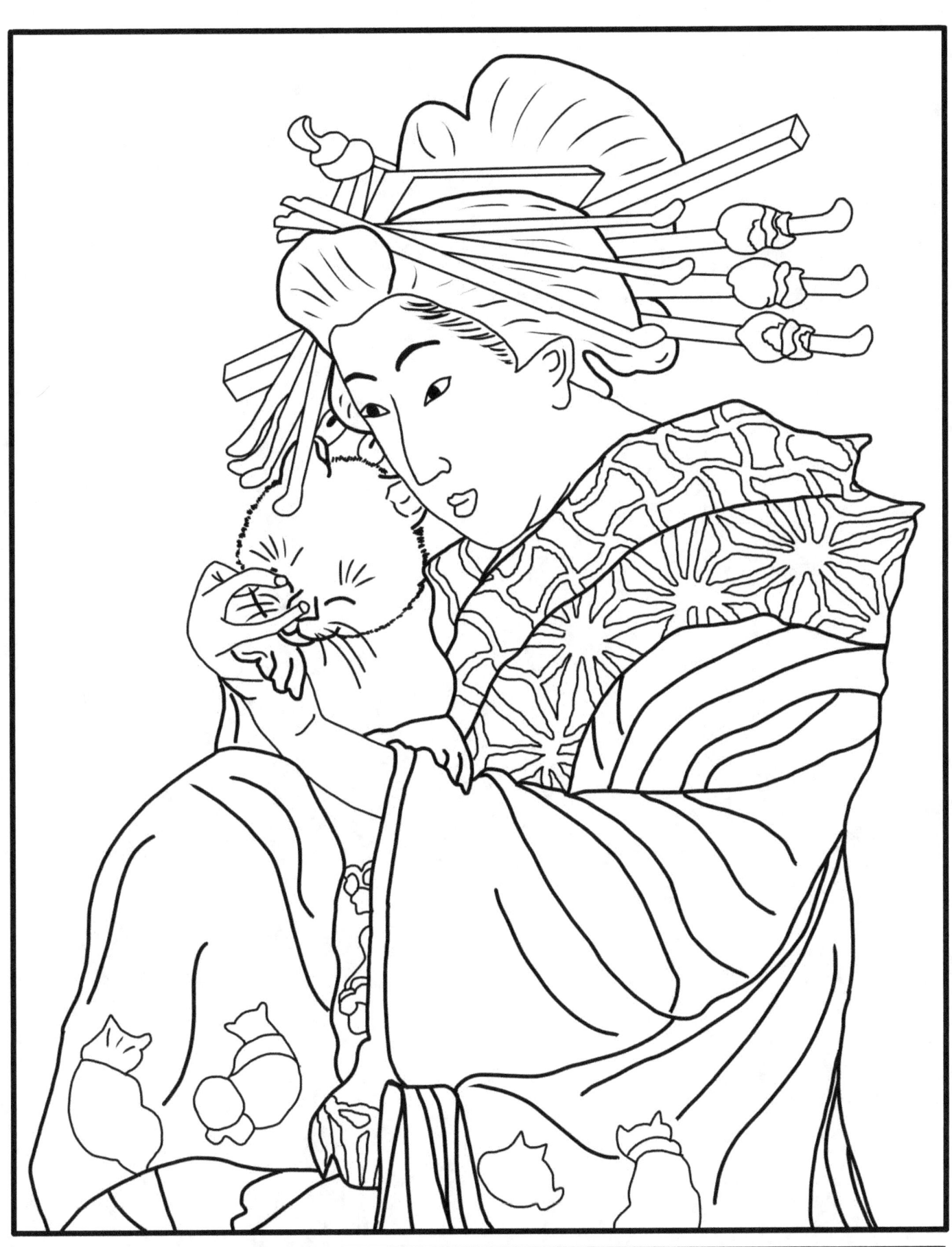

Courtesan Usugumo and her cat Ukiyo-e woodblock print from Mirror of Beauties Past and Present, Taiso Yoshitoshi, 1875-1876

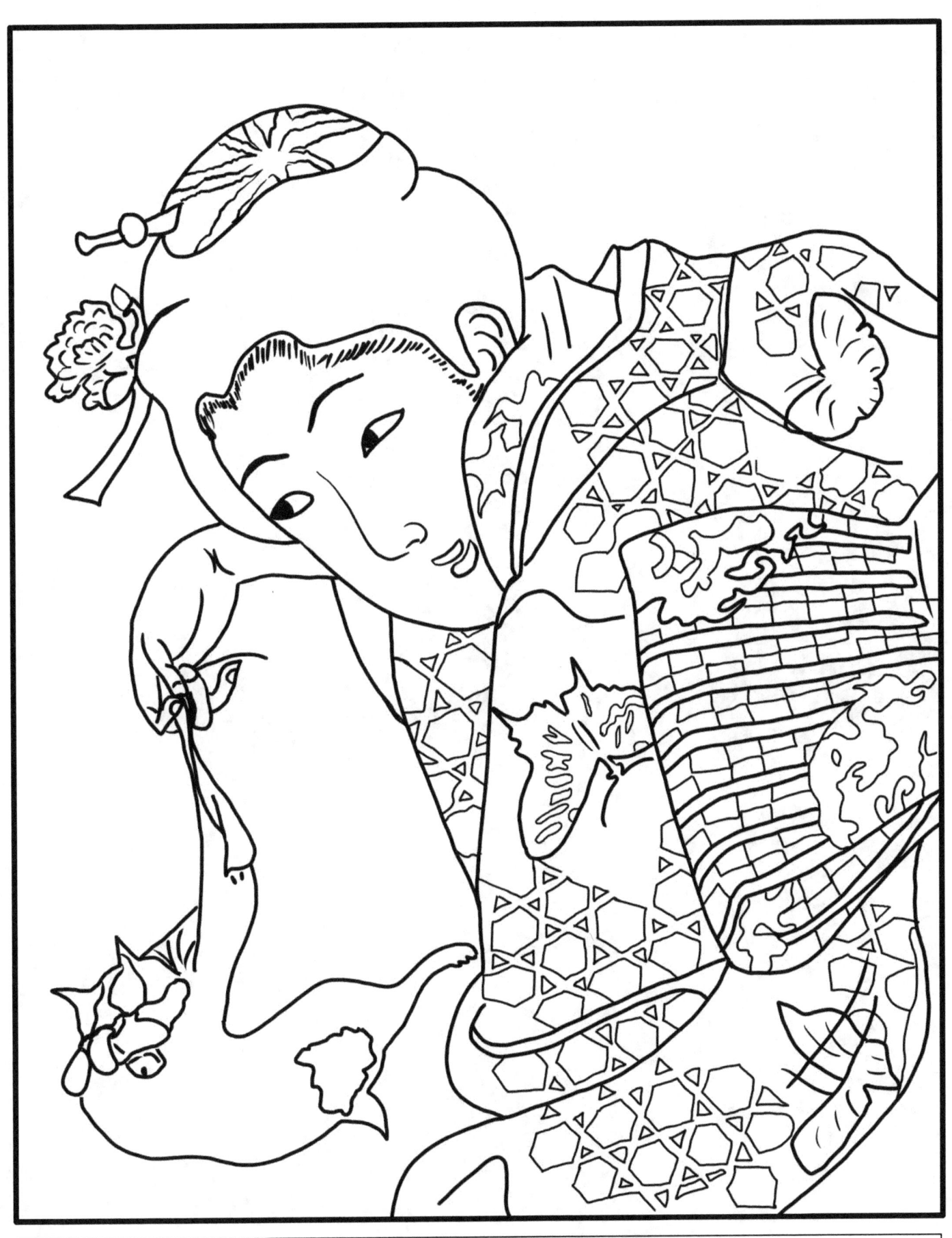

TRUE BEAUTIES, CHIKANOBU TOYOHARA

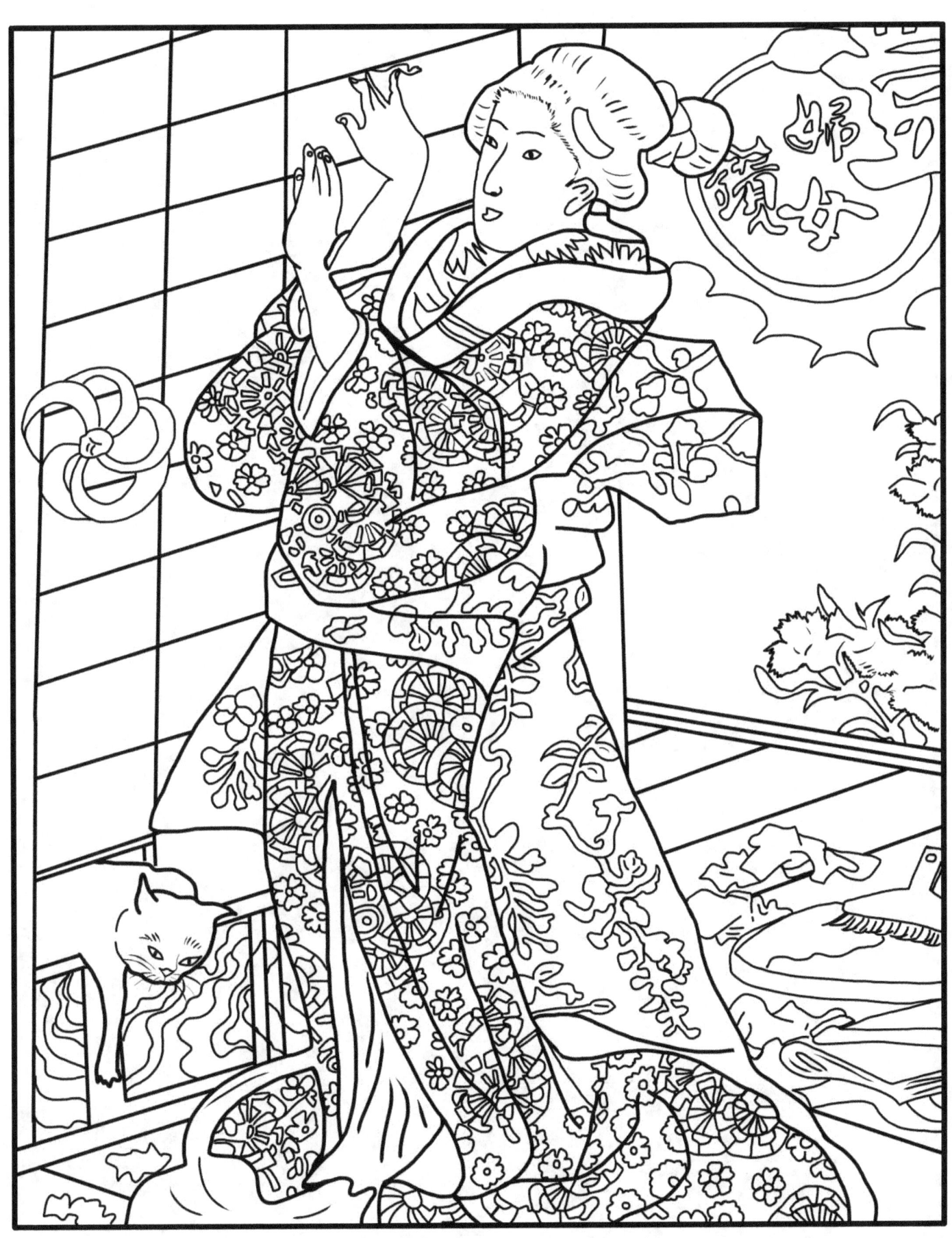

Cat Destroying Rice Paper, Utagawa Kuniyoshi

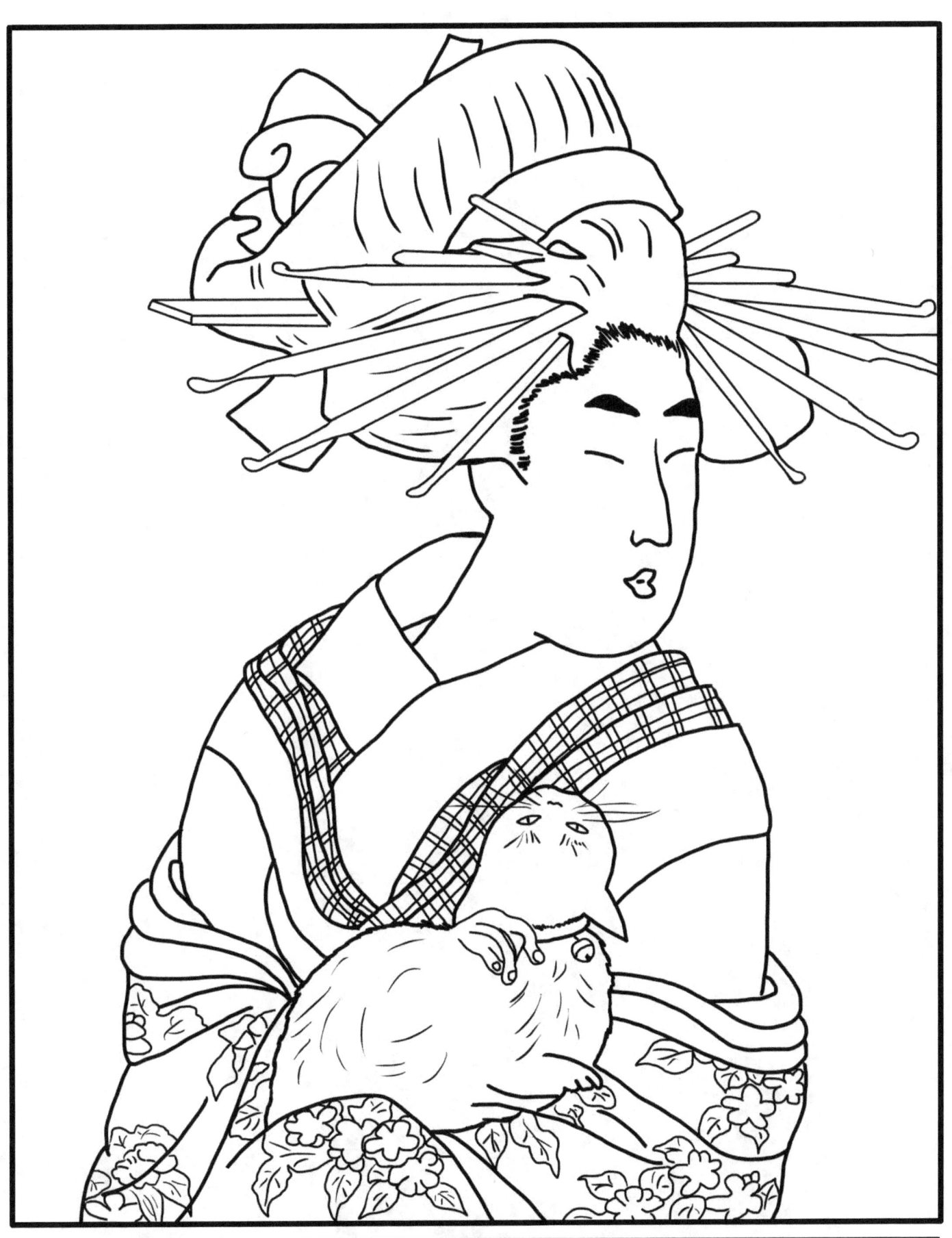

GEISHA HOLDING CAT, KITAGAWA UTAMARO

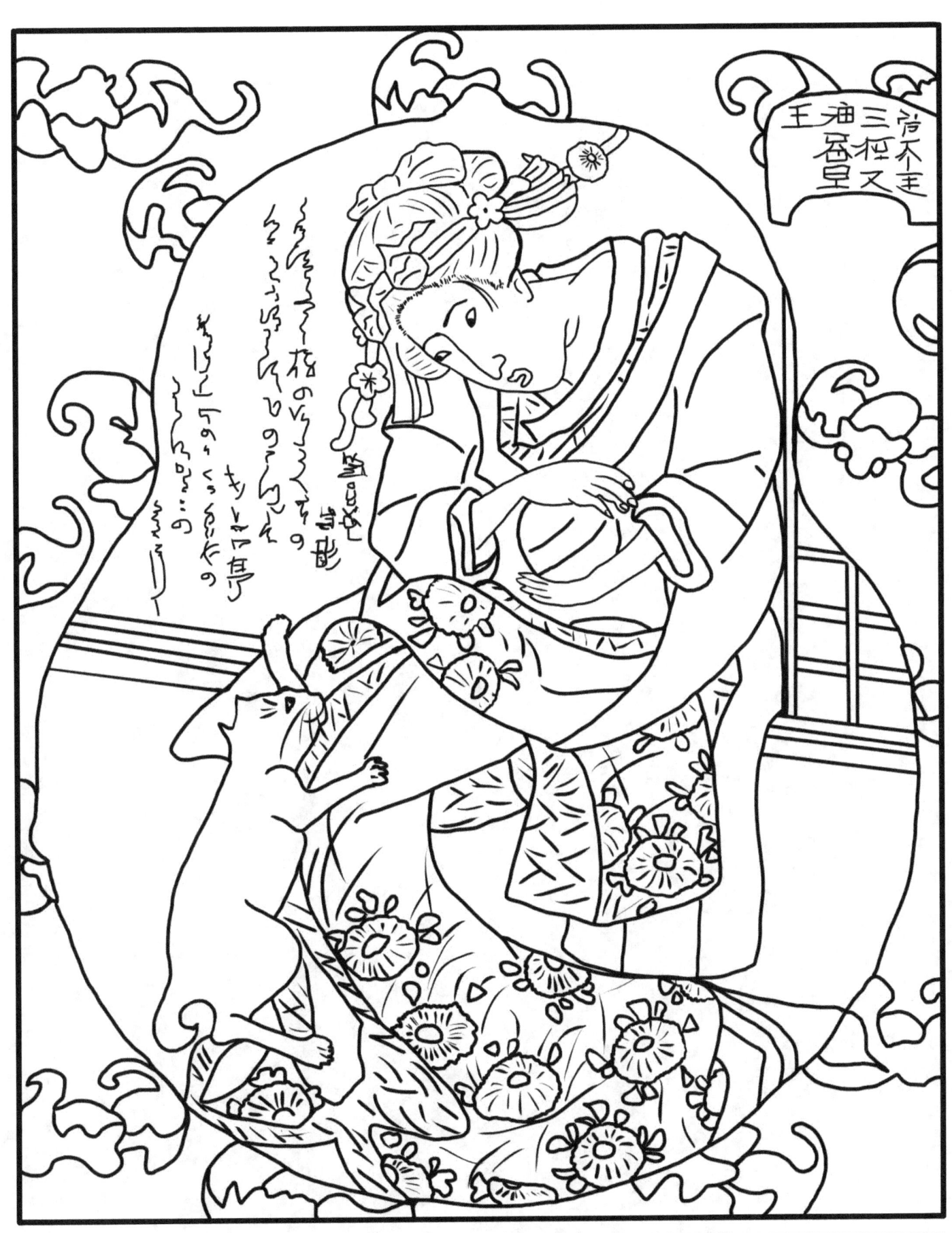

Cat Wanting Attention, Utagawa Sadakage

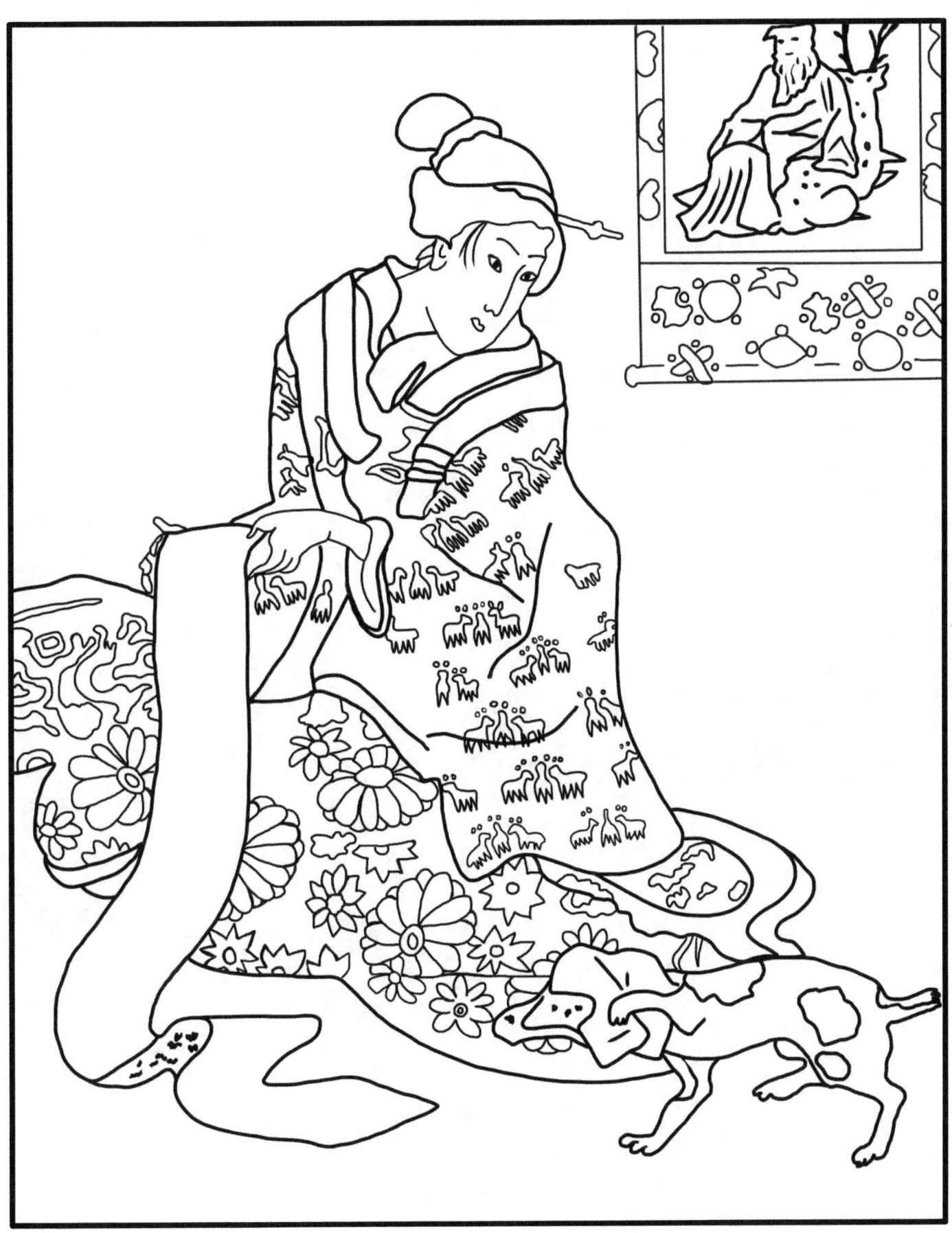

BAKENEKO, UTAGAWA KUNIYOSHI

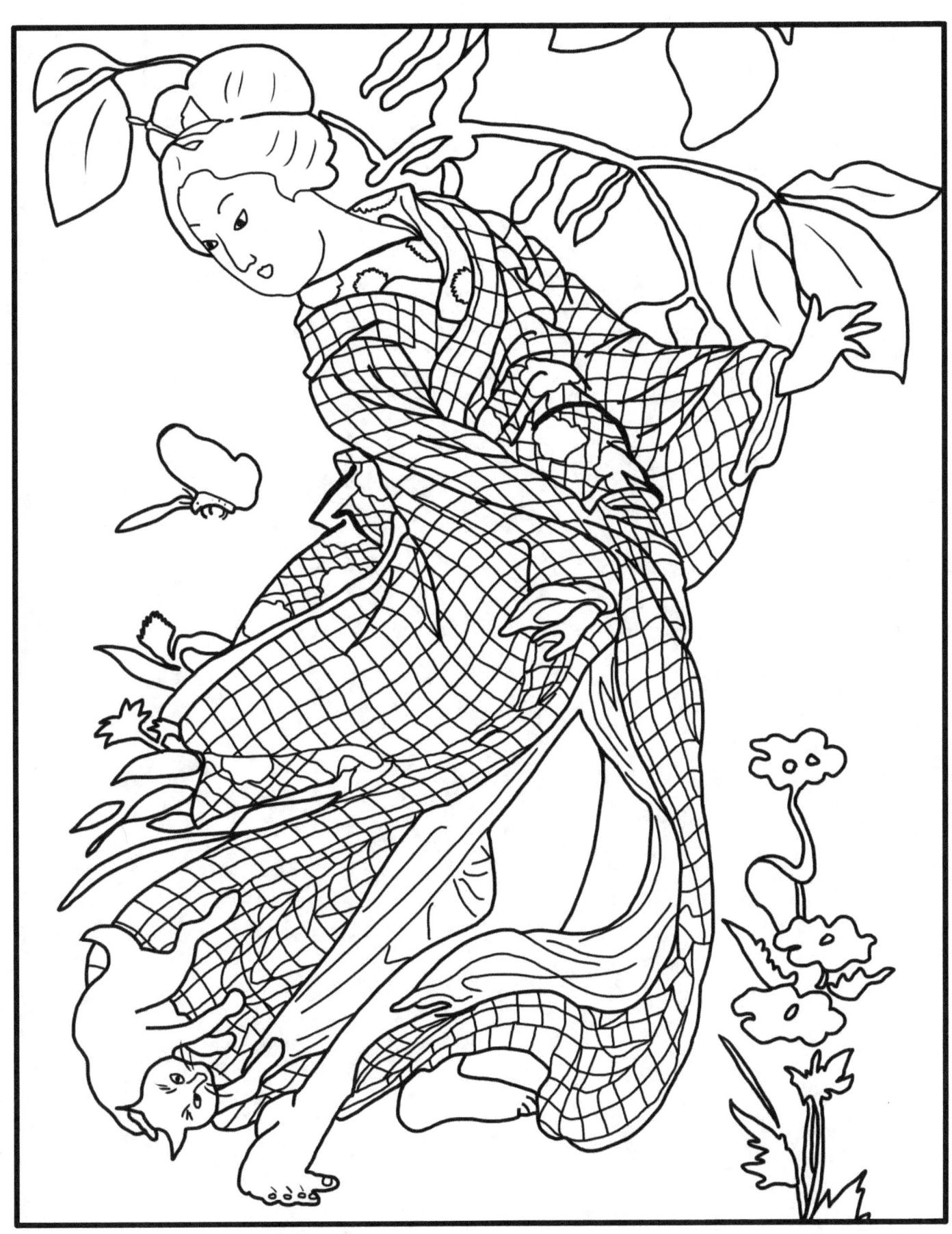

Ukiyo-e Cat and Geisha, Anon.

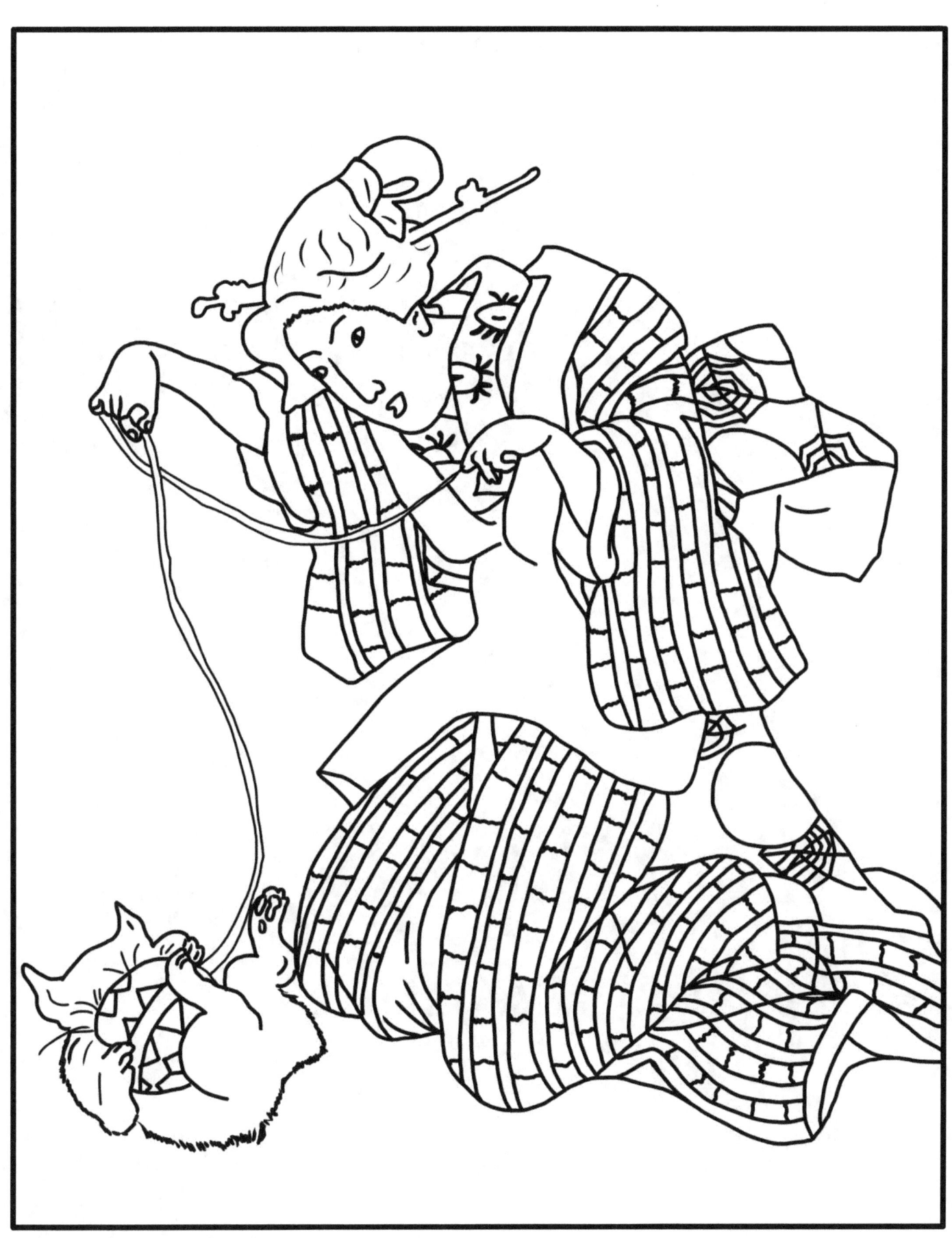

GEISHA PLAYING WITH A CAT WITH STRING, UTAGAWA KUNITOSHI

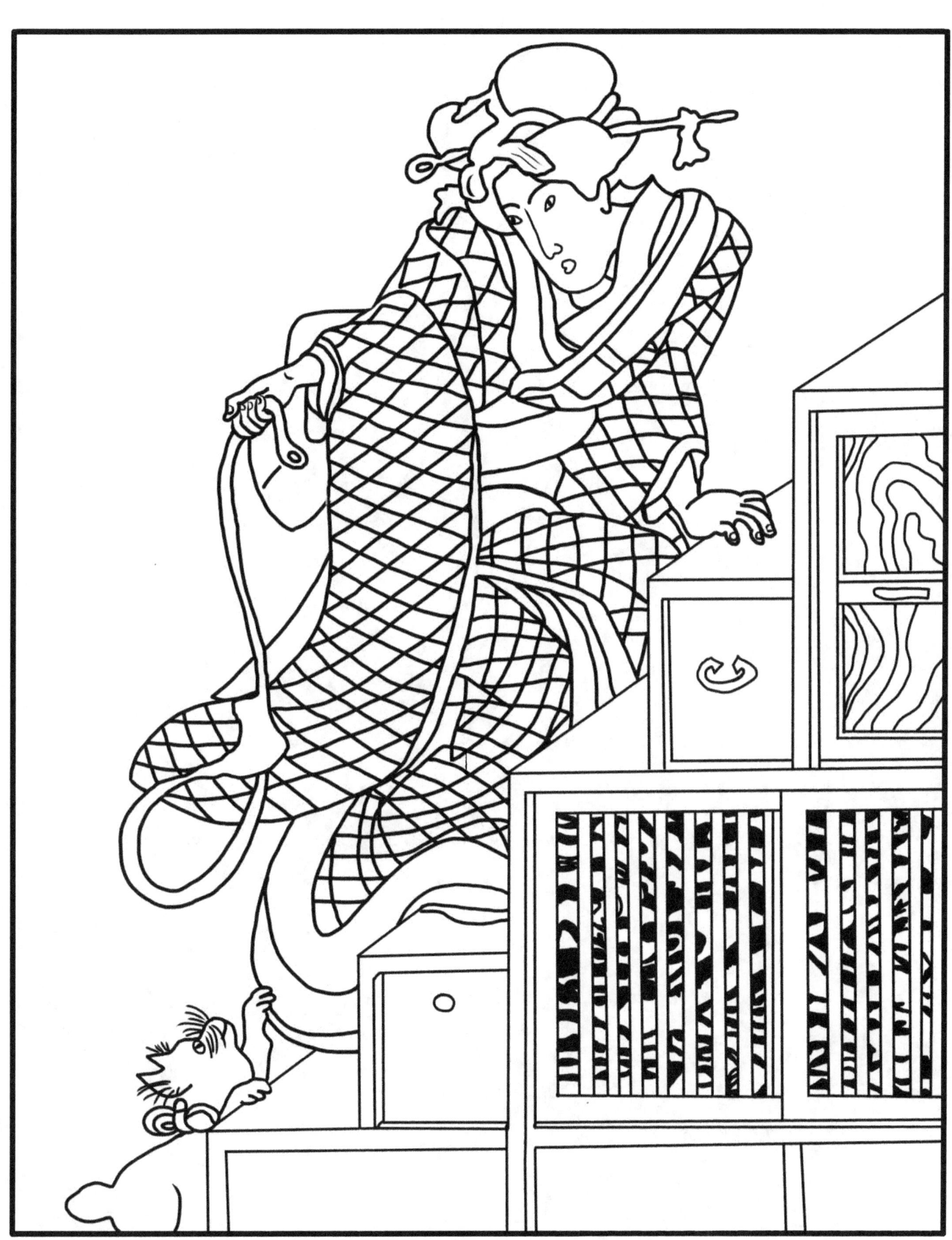

GEISHA TEASING A CAT, UTAGAWA KUNISADA

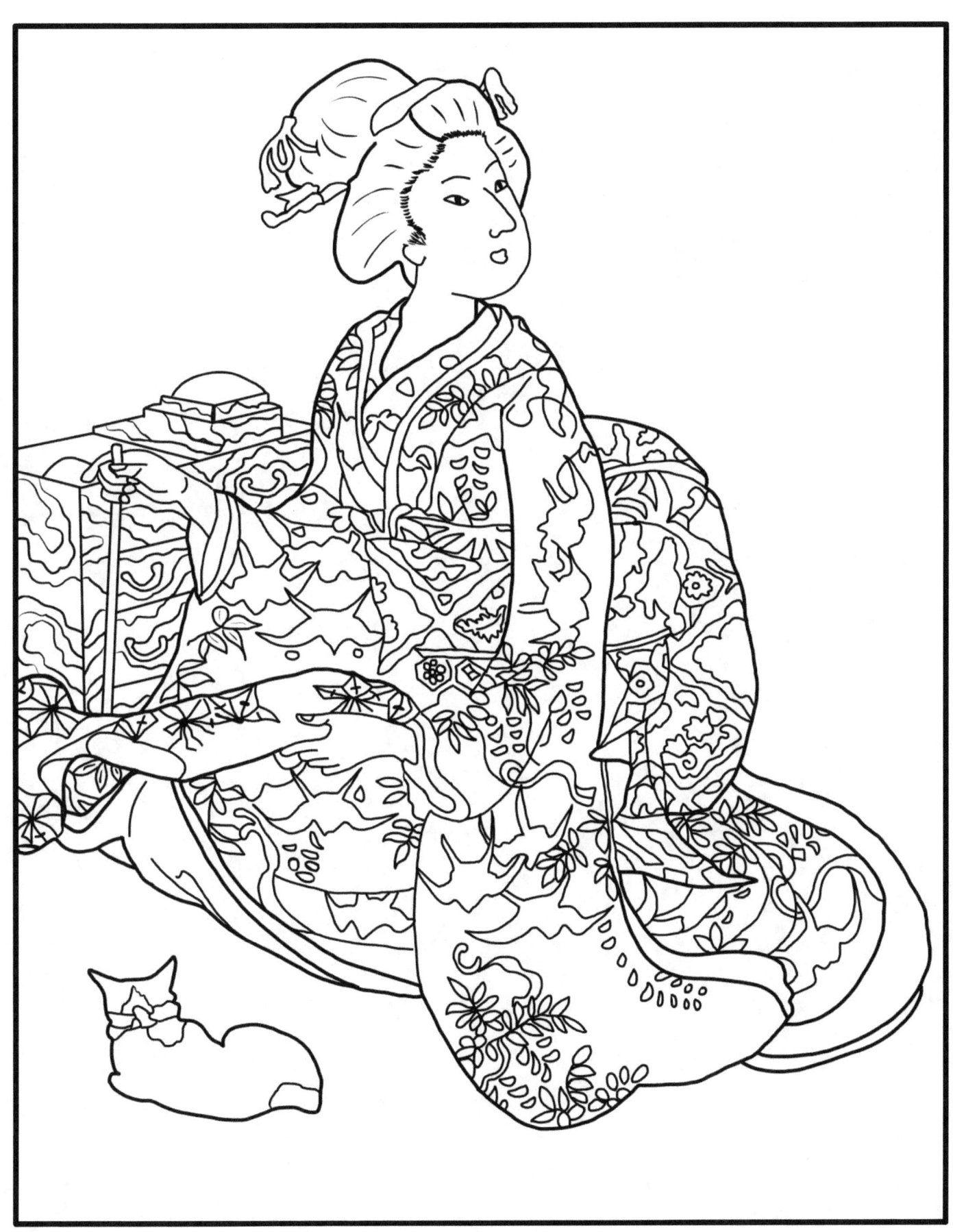

Seamstress and Cat, Ukiyo-e Period, Anon.

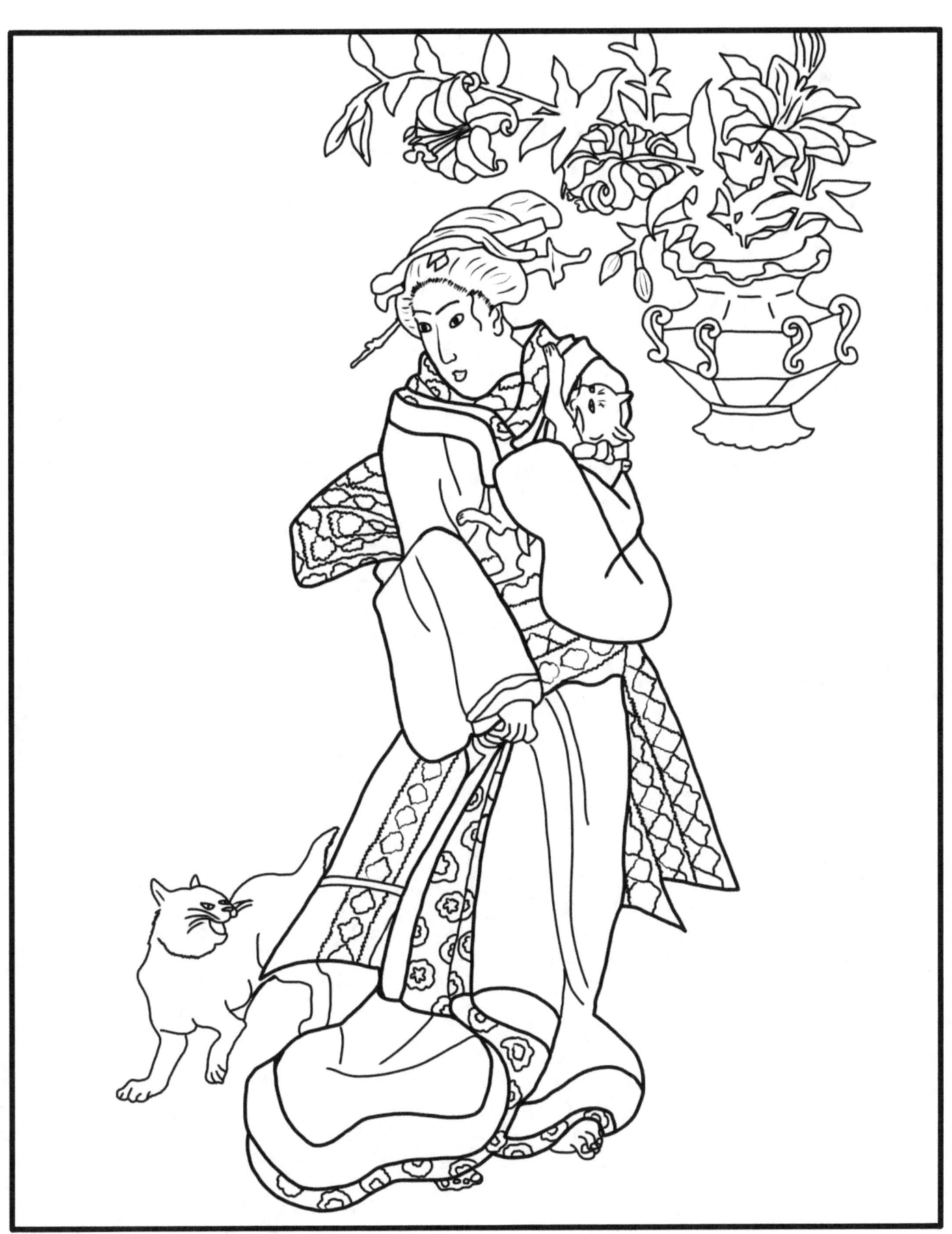

GEISHA AND TWO CATS, UTAGAWA KUNIYOSHI

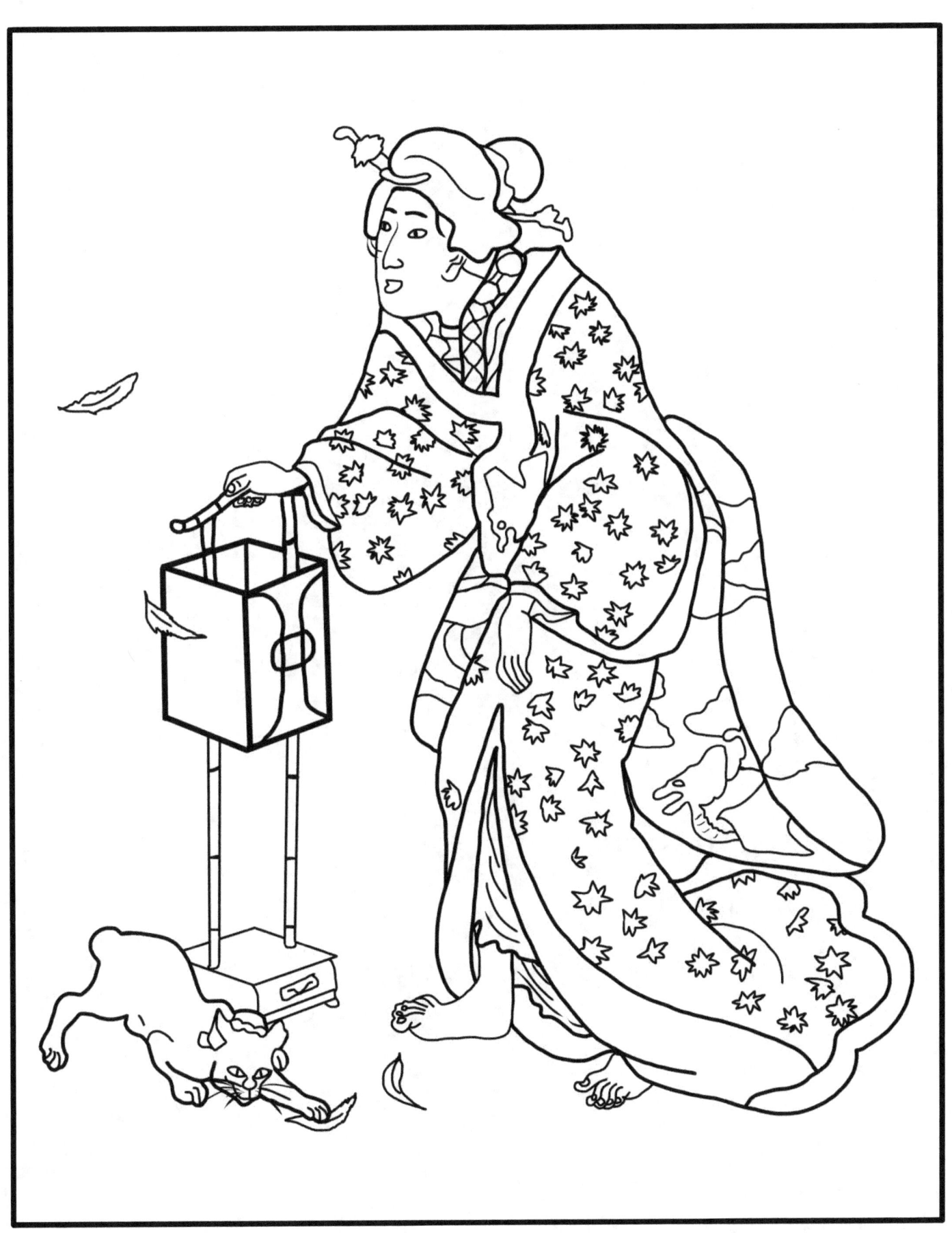

BUN'YA NO YASUHIDE FROM THE SERIES PARODIES OF THE SIX POETIC IMMORTALS,
UTAGAWA KUNISADA, 1848-54

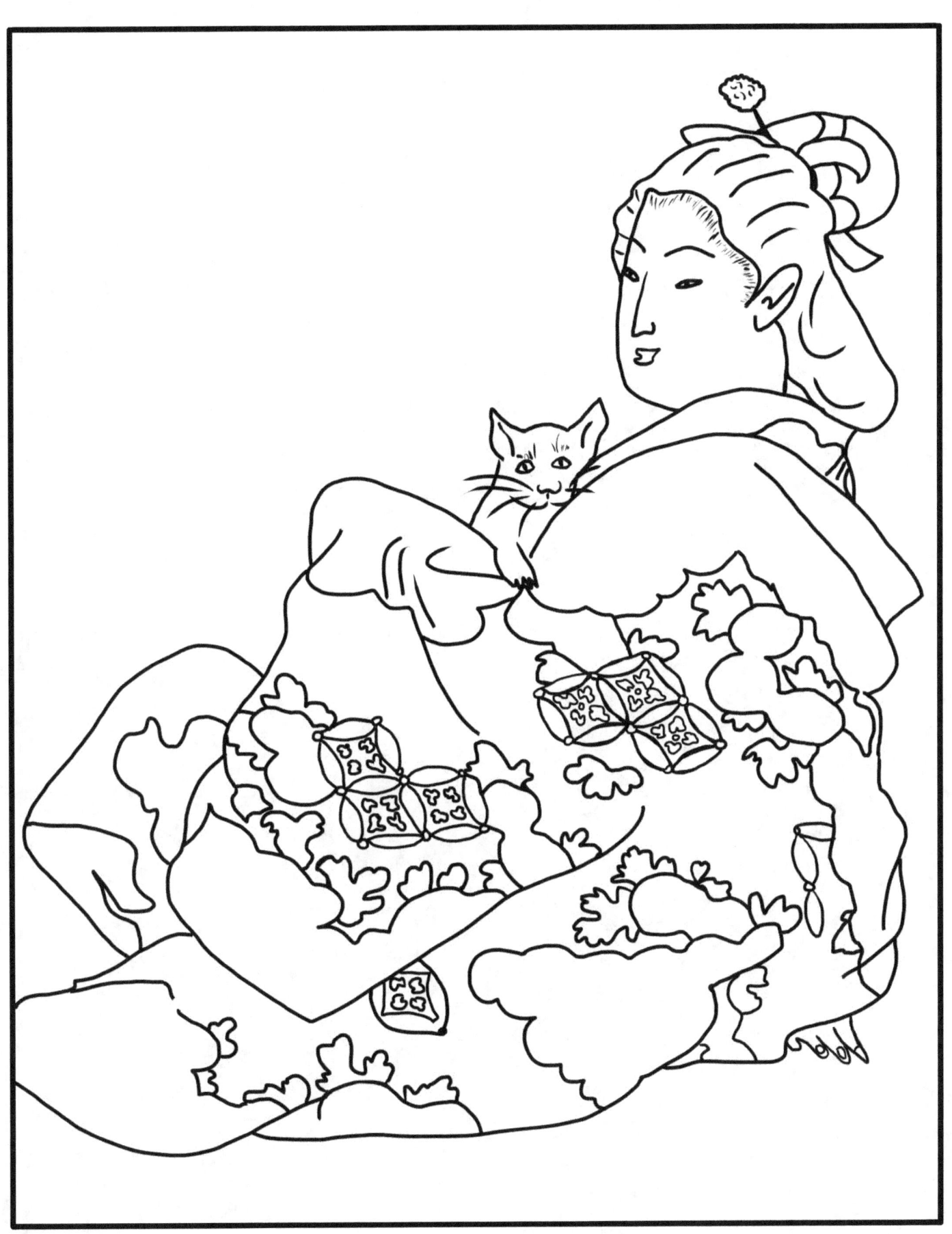

Young Beauty and Cat, Ogata Gekko, ca. 1888

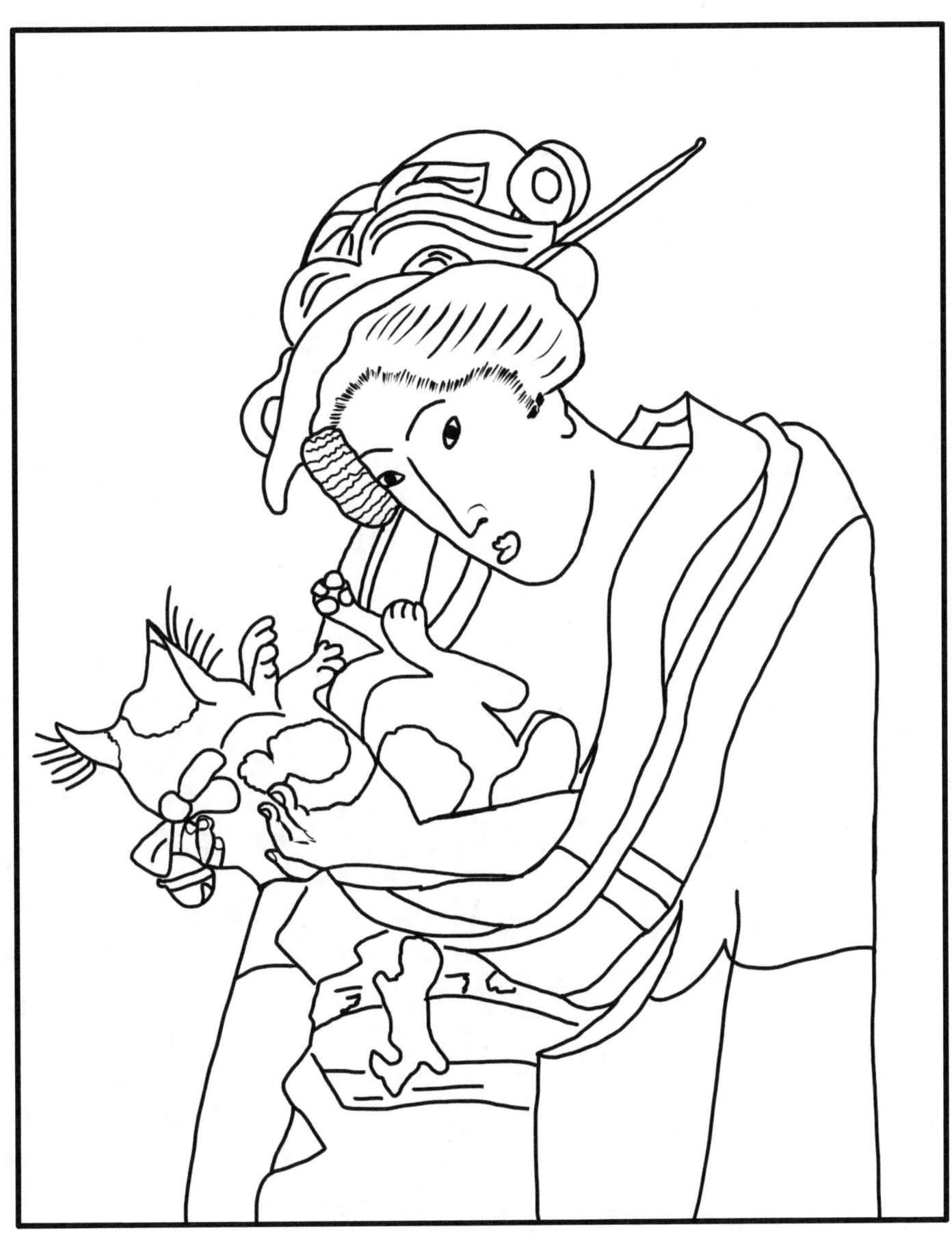

GEISHA HOLDING A CAT, UTAGAWA KUNISADA

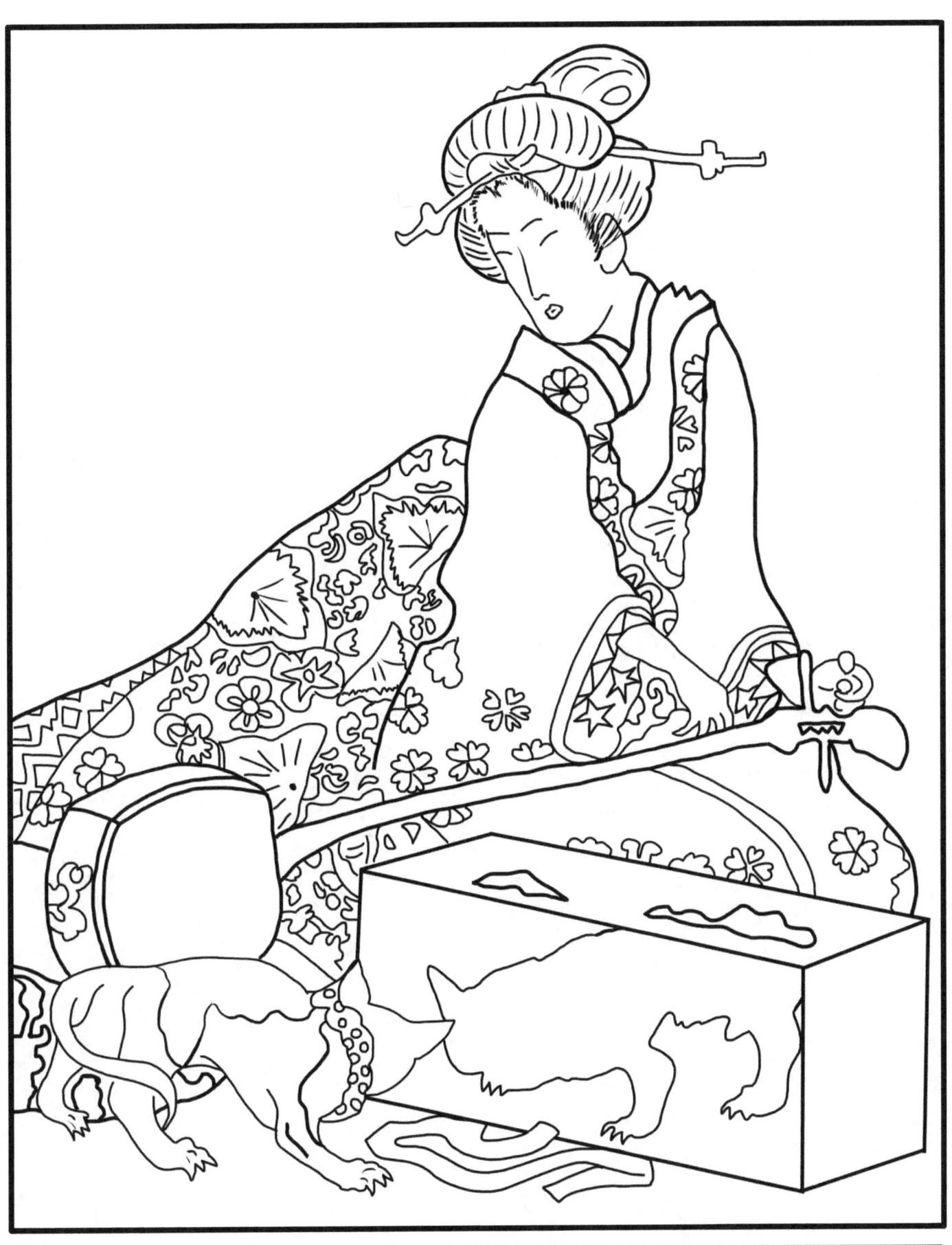

Woman Tuning a Shamisen and a Cat Looking at its Own Reflection,

Yashima Gakutei, mid~ 1820

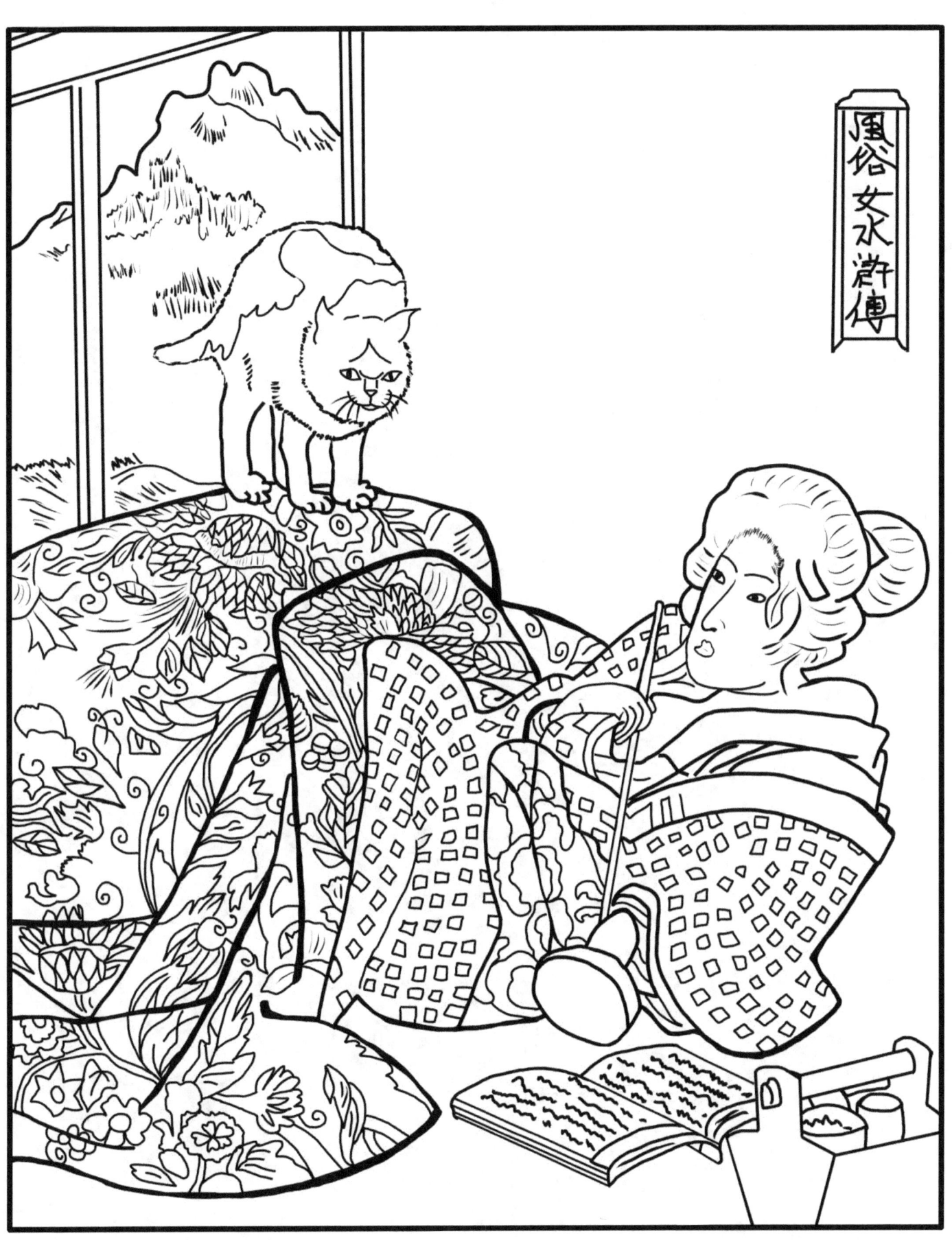

風俗女水滸傳

Kamenoya Osamaru, Hisakataya, Utagawa Kuniyoshi, 1832

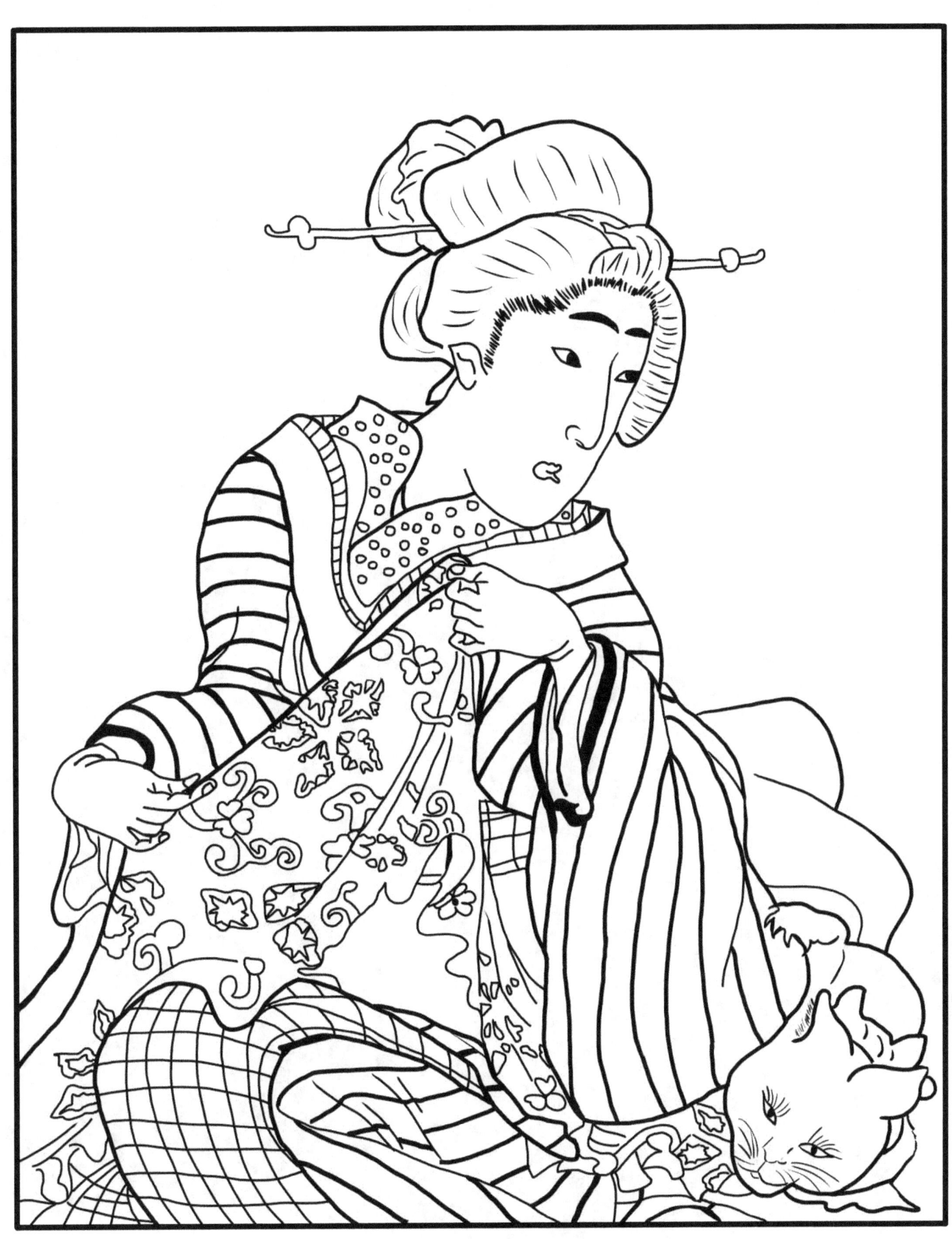

Cat and Geisha, Toyohara Kunichika

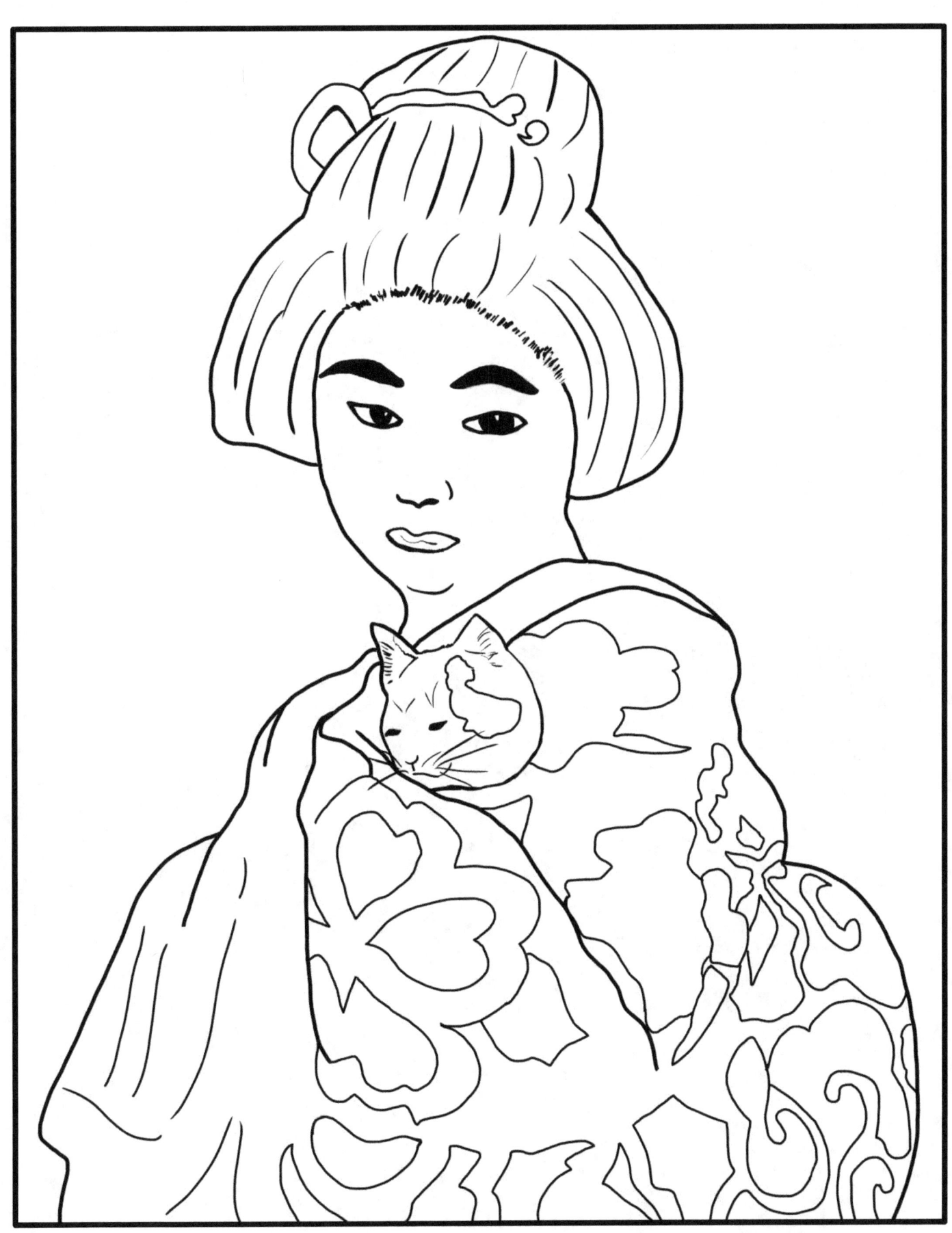

GEISHA AND CAT, ANON.

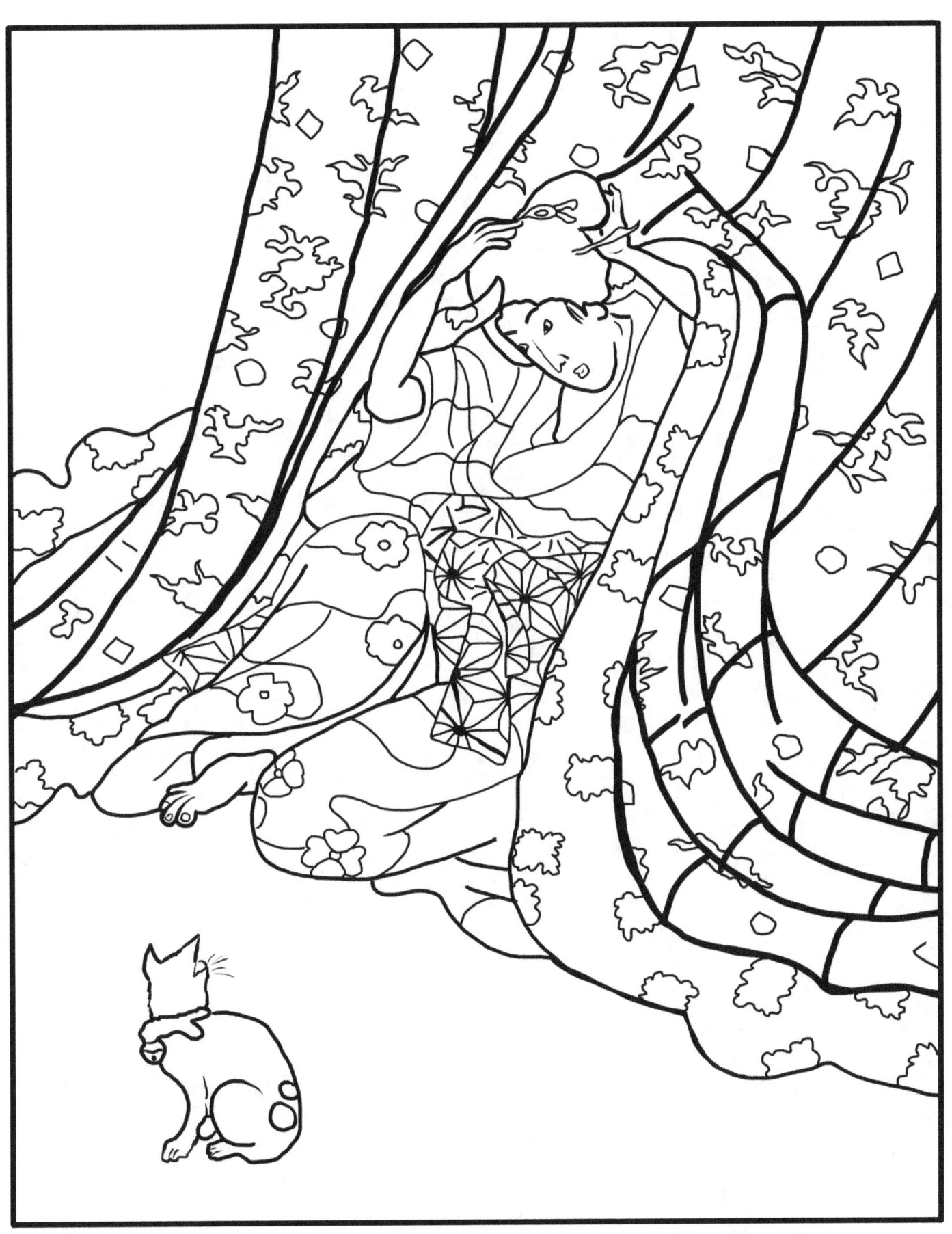

COURTESAN BENEATH A MOSQUITO NET, UTAGAWA KUNISADA, 1855

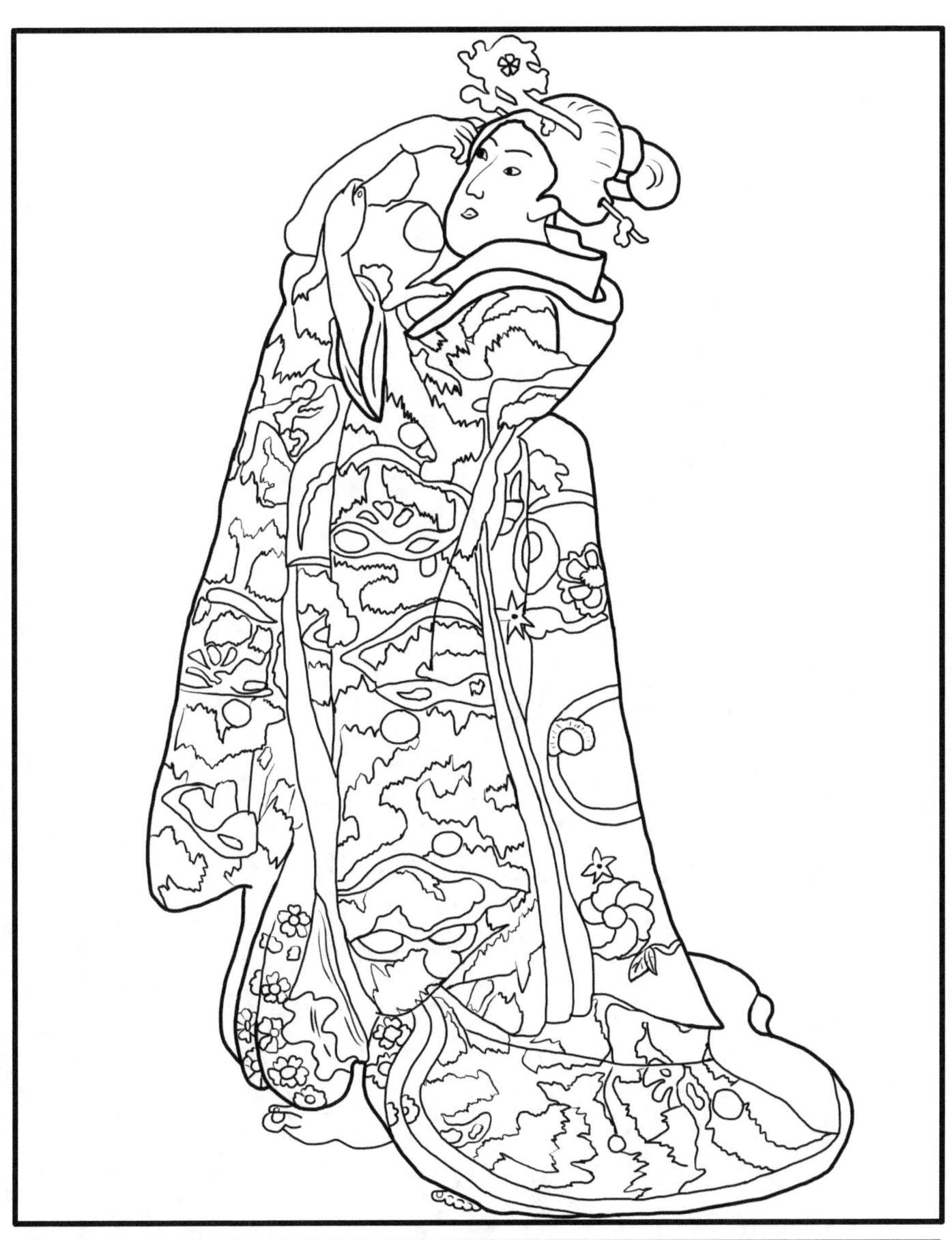

GEISHA WITH CAT OVER HER SHOULDER, UTAGAWA KUNIYOSHI

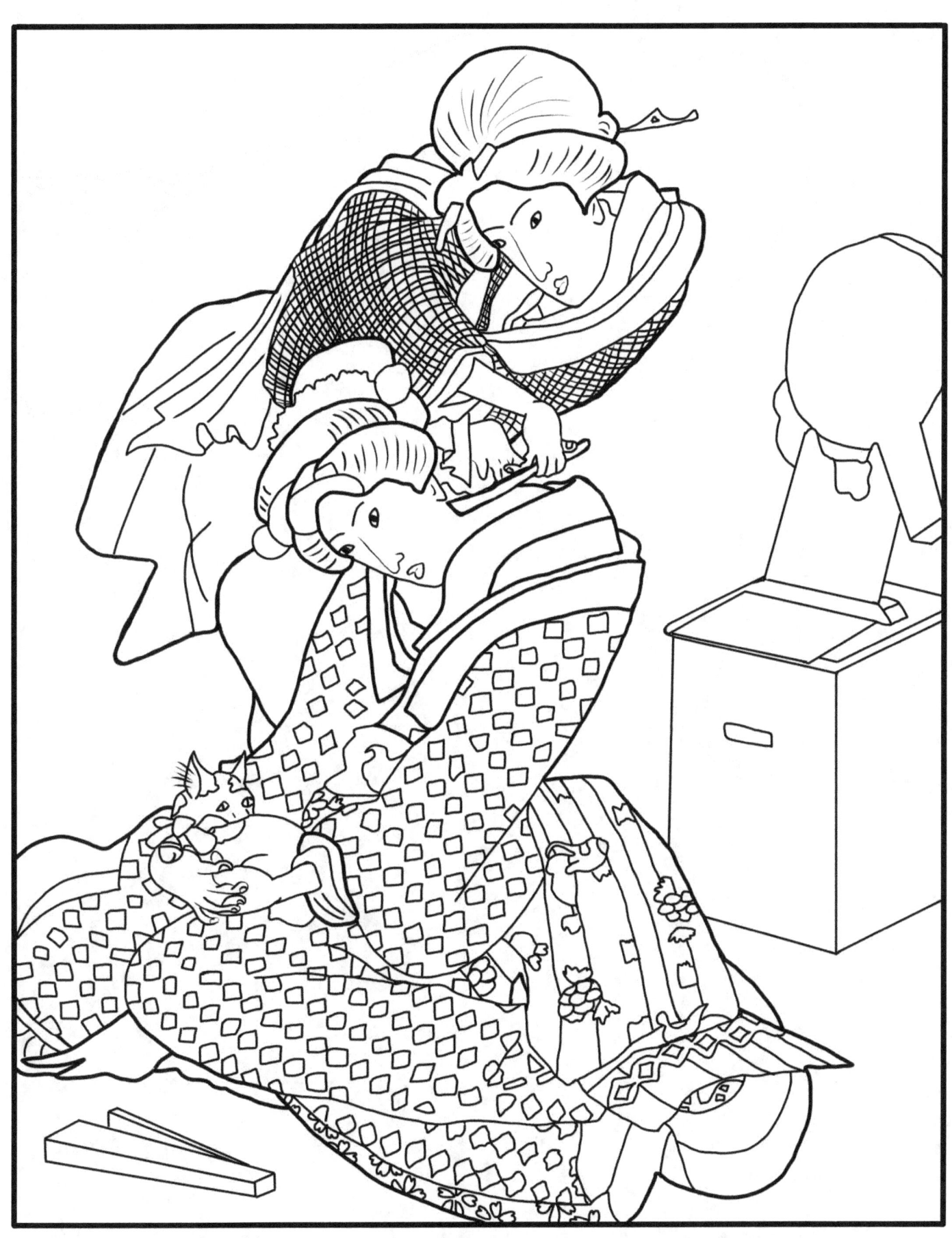

Shaving the Nape of the Neck, Utagawa Kunisada

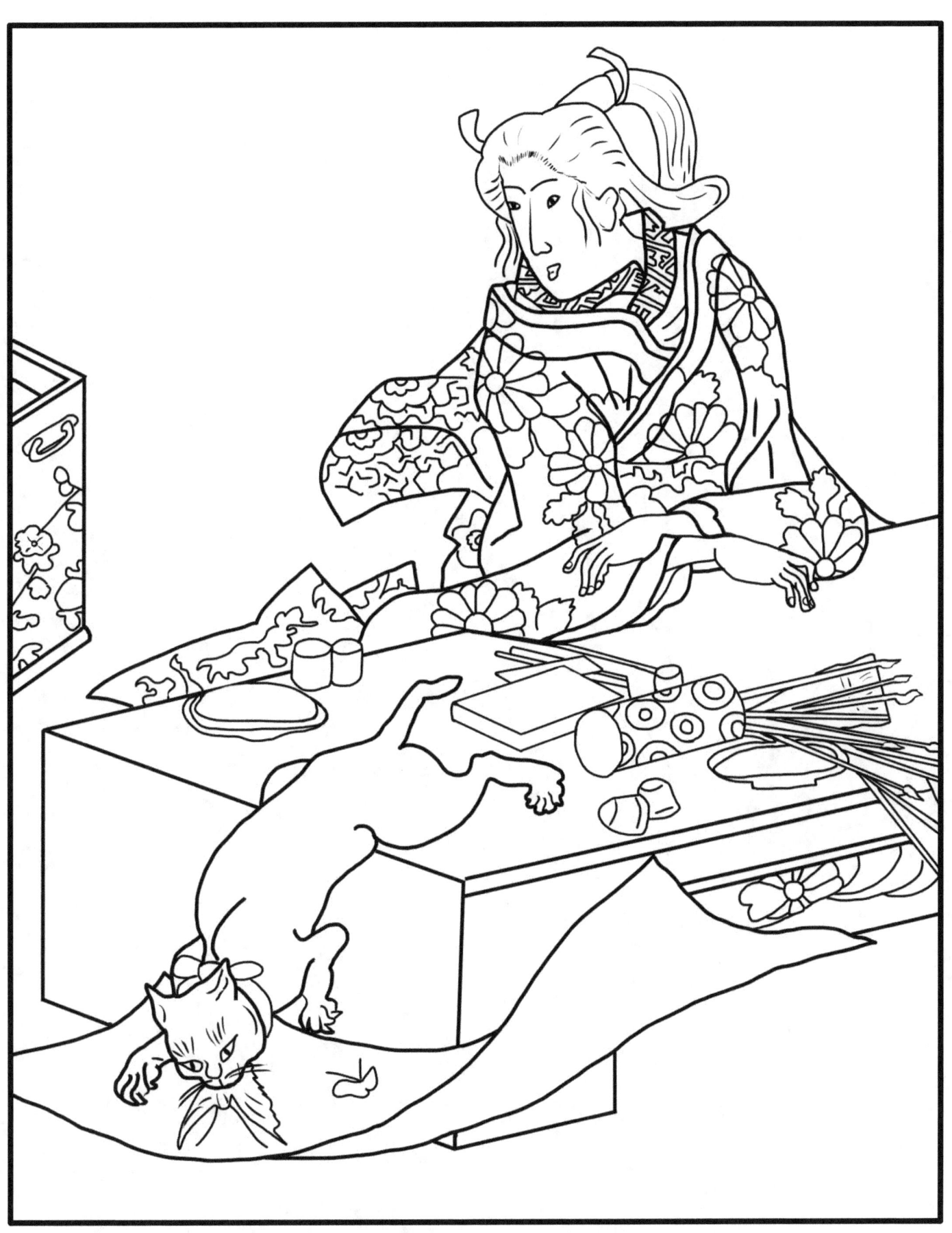

Cat Catching a Butterfly, Utagawa Kuniyoshi, mid 1840s

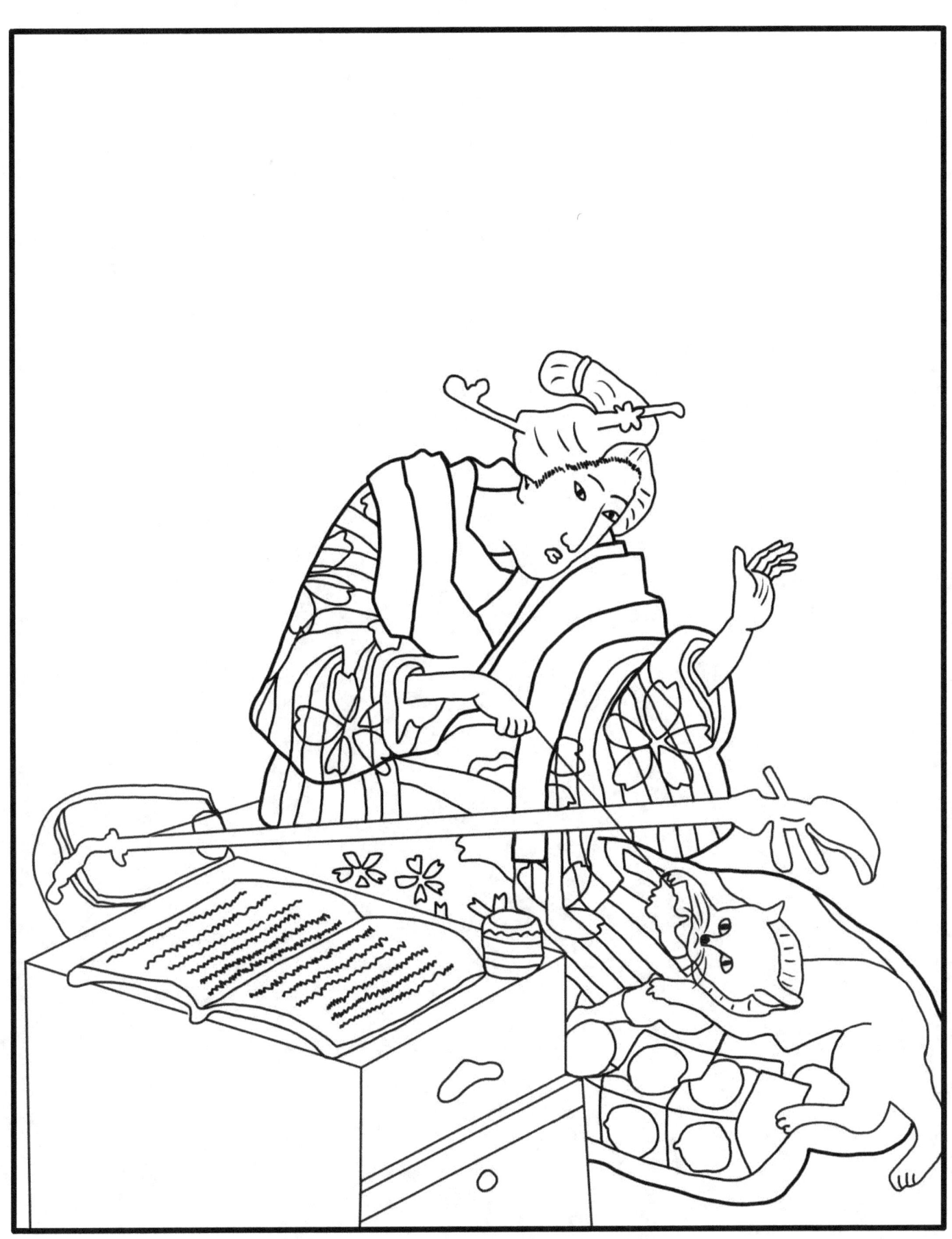

Cat Playing with a String, Utagawa Sadatora

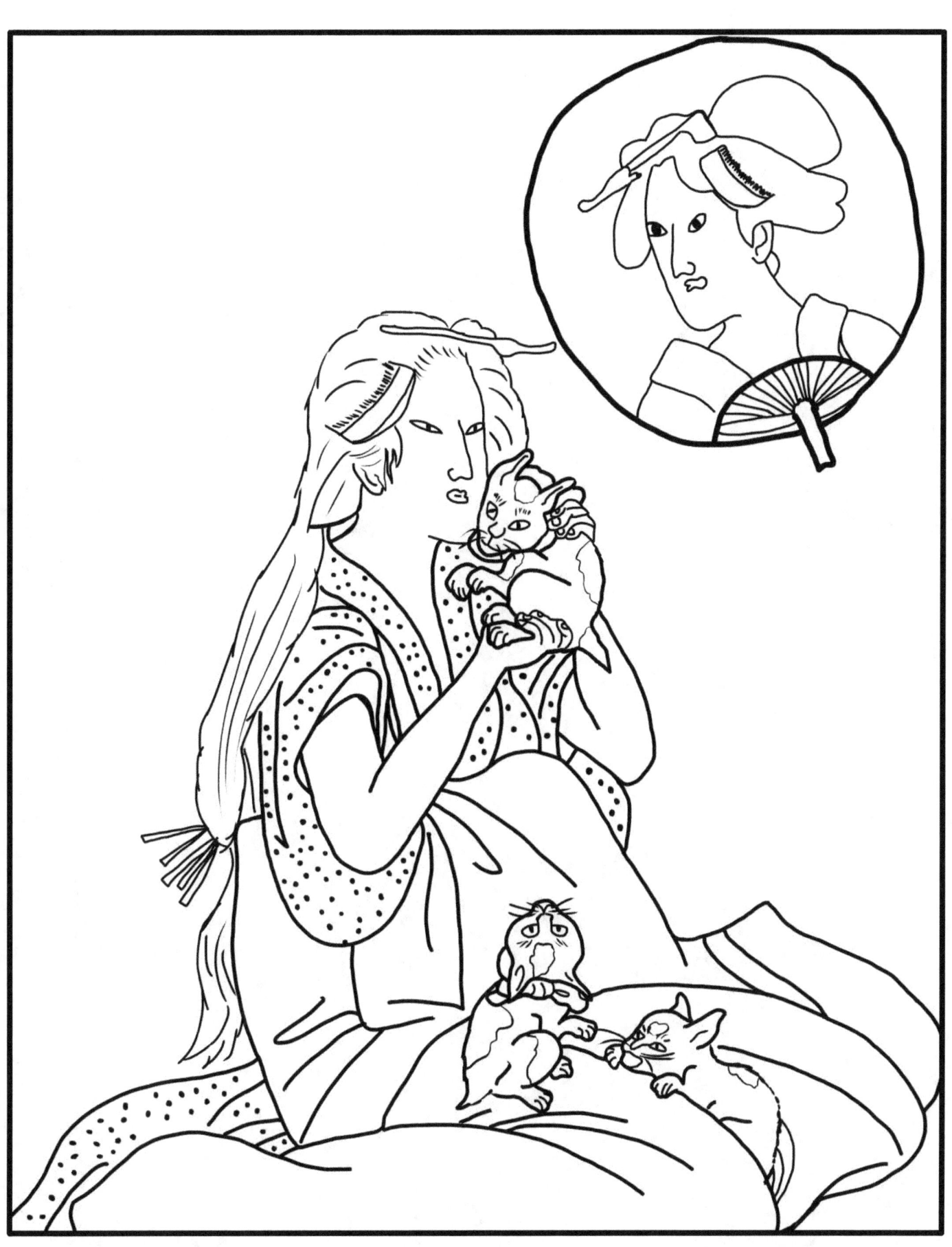

WOMAN HOLDING A CAT, UKIYO-E WOODBLOCK PRINT, EARLY 19TH CENTURY, ANON.

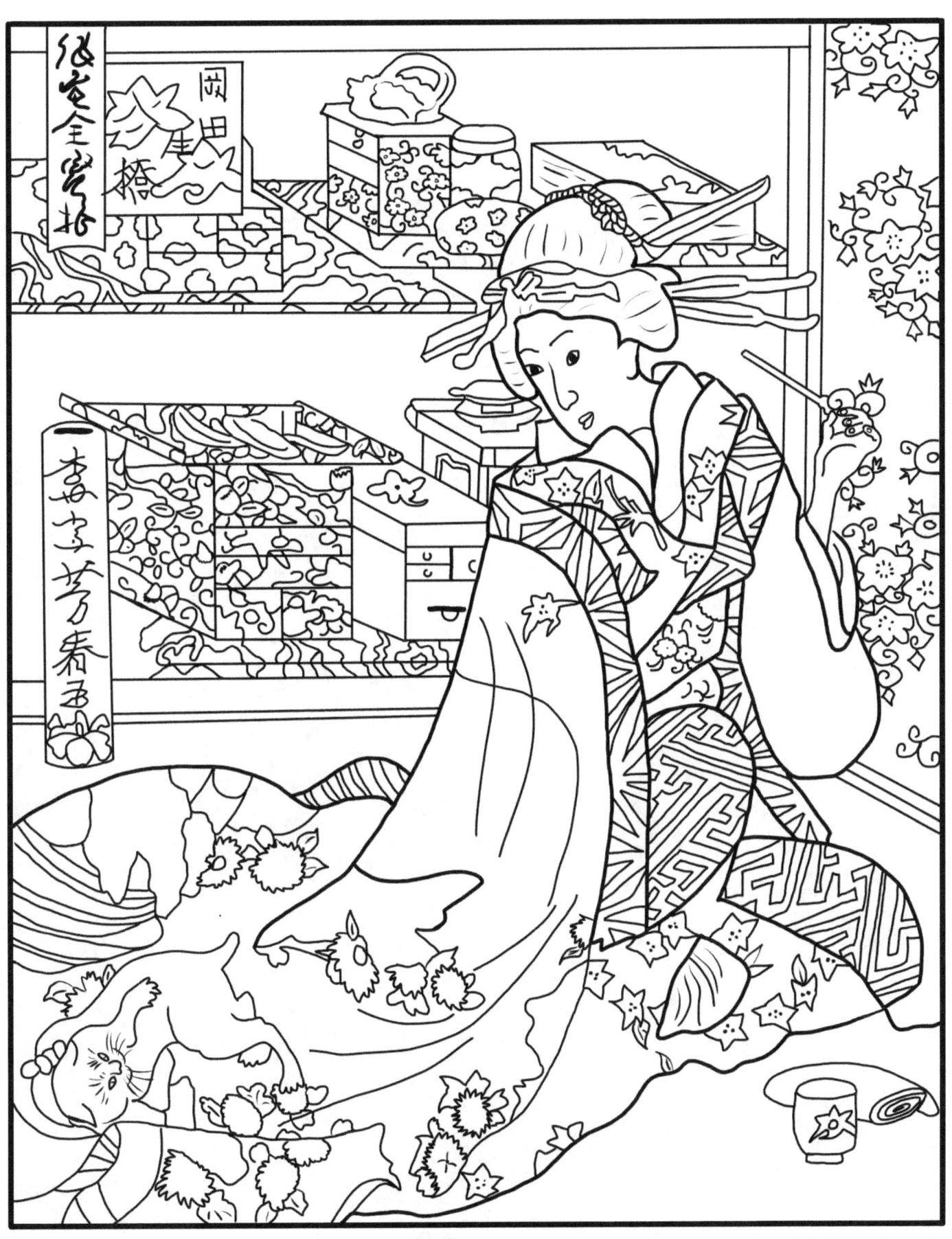

Cat Playing with a Geisha's dress, Ukiyo-e woodblock print, Early 19th century

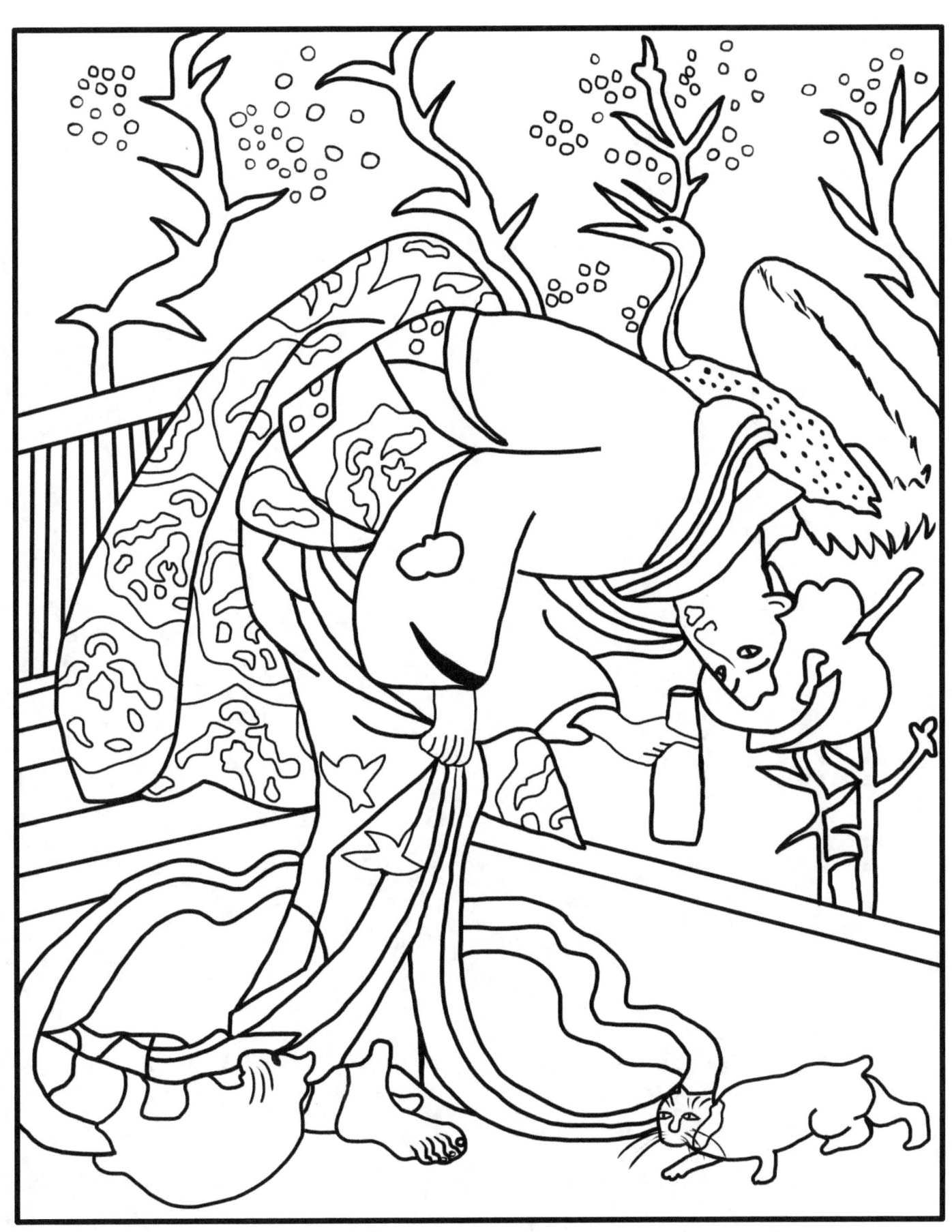

GEISHA FEEDING CATS, UTAGAWA KUNIYOSHI

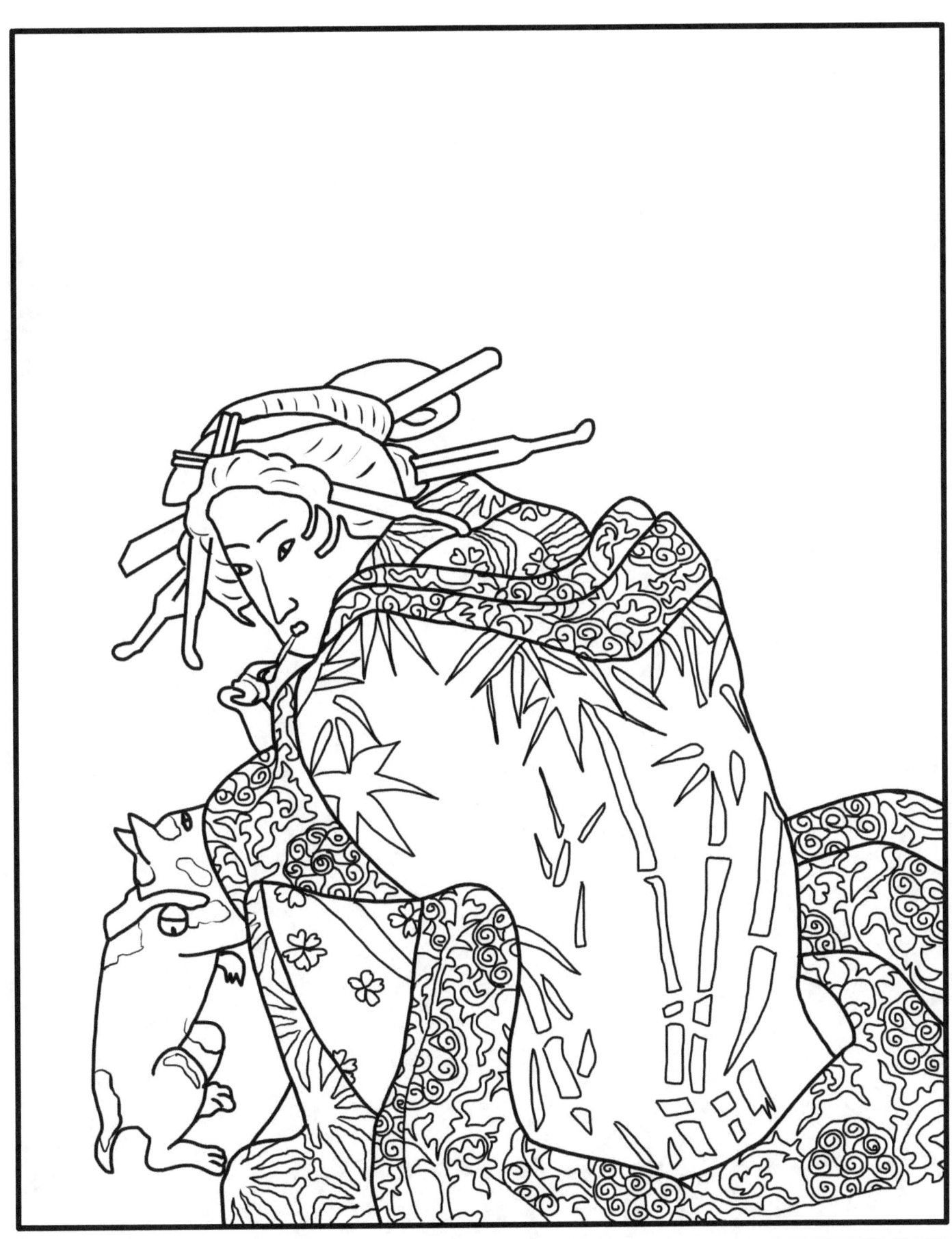

GEISHA SITTING WITH CAT, UTAGAWA TOYOKUNI

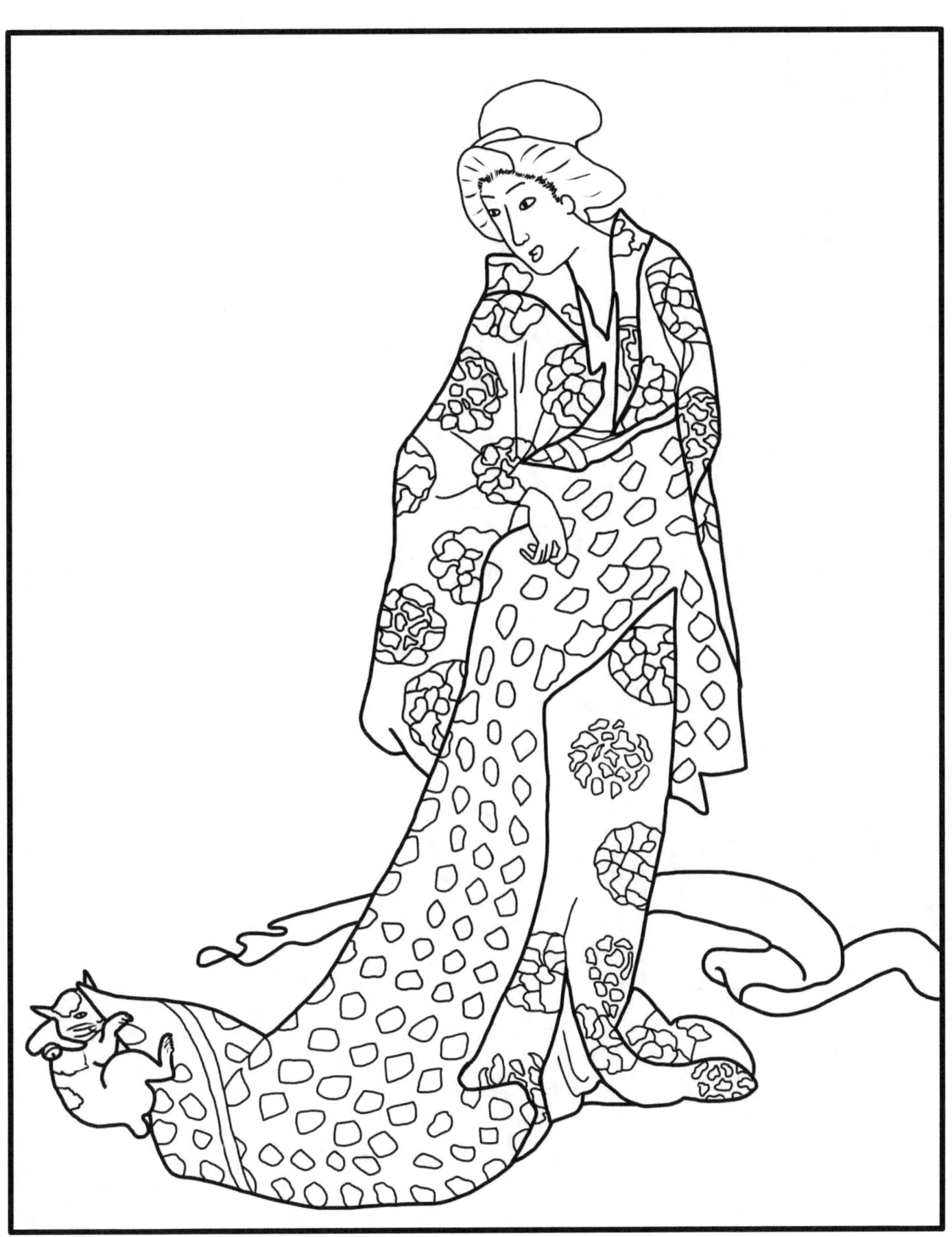

Utagawa Kuniyoshi (1797-1862)

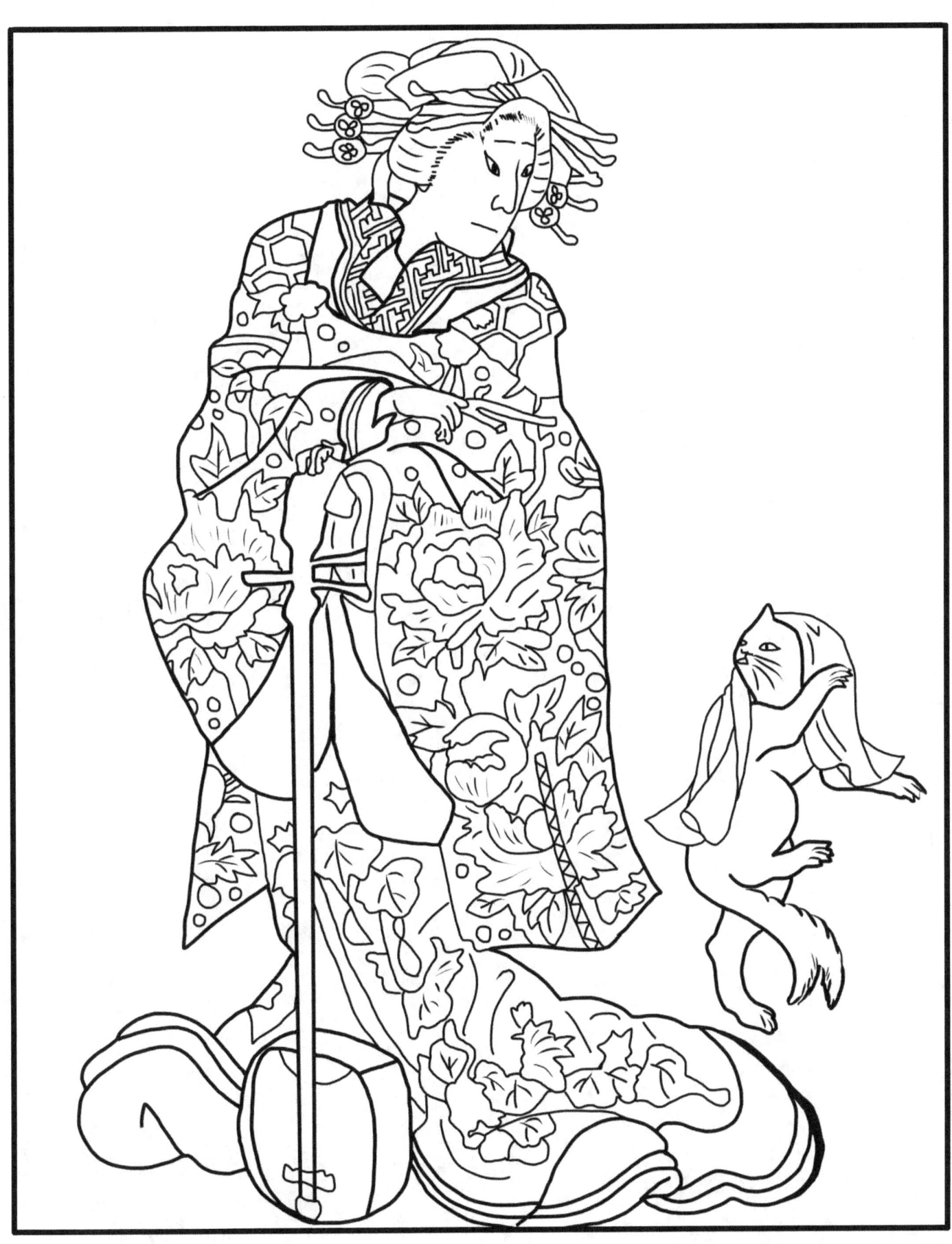

ACTOR ICHIKAWA UDANJI I AS THE COURTESAN MICHINOKU AND CAT,

UTAGAWA YOSHITAKI

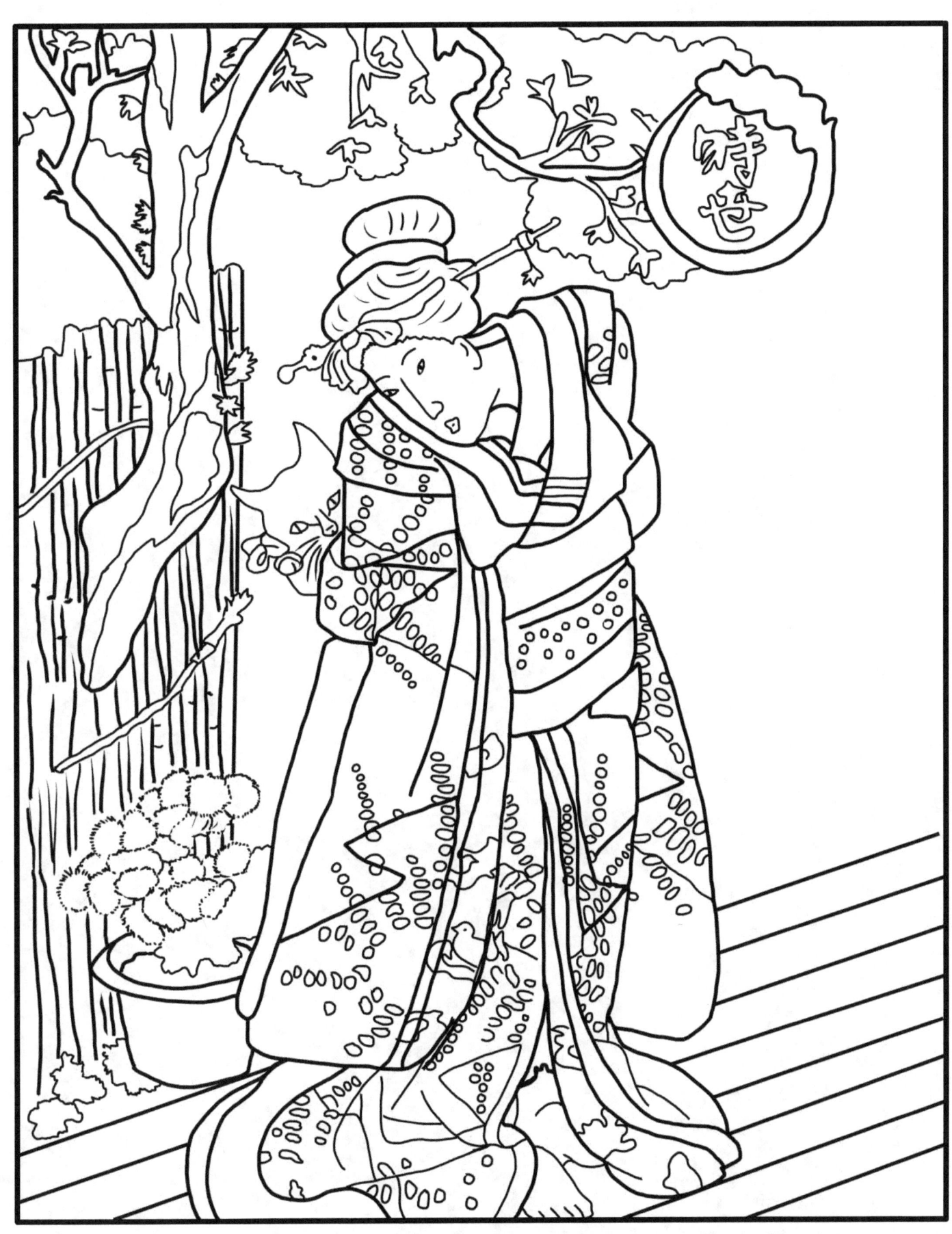

Beauty Playing with a Cat, Toyokuni Kunisada (1786 - 1860)

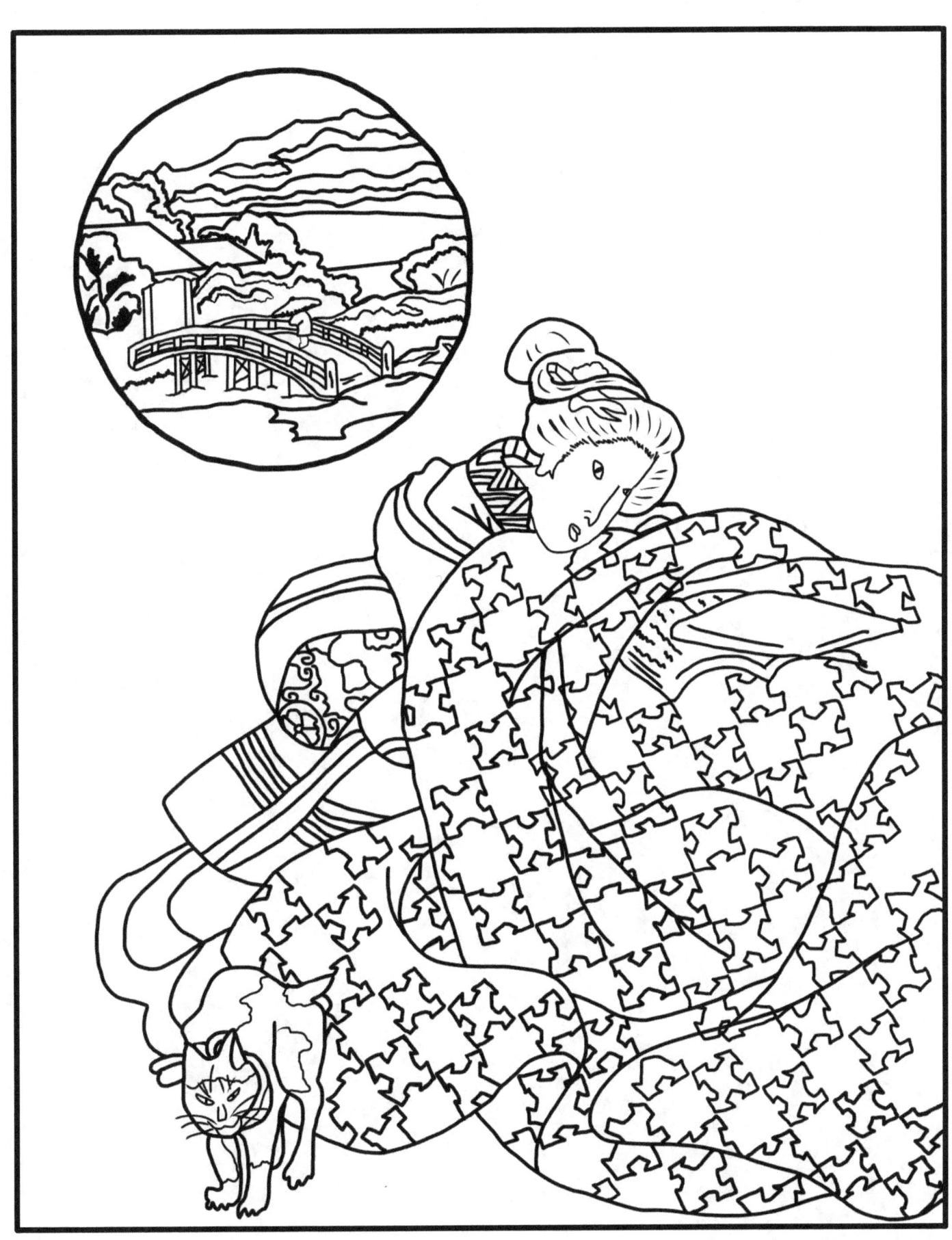

Twilight Snow at Shin Dote, Utagawa Toyokuni II

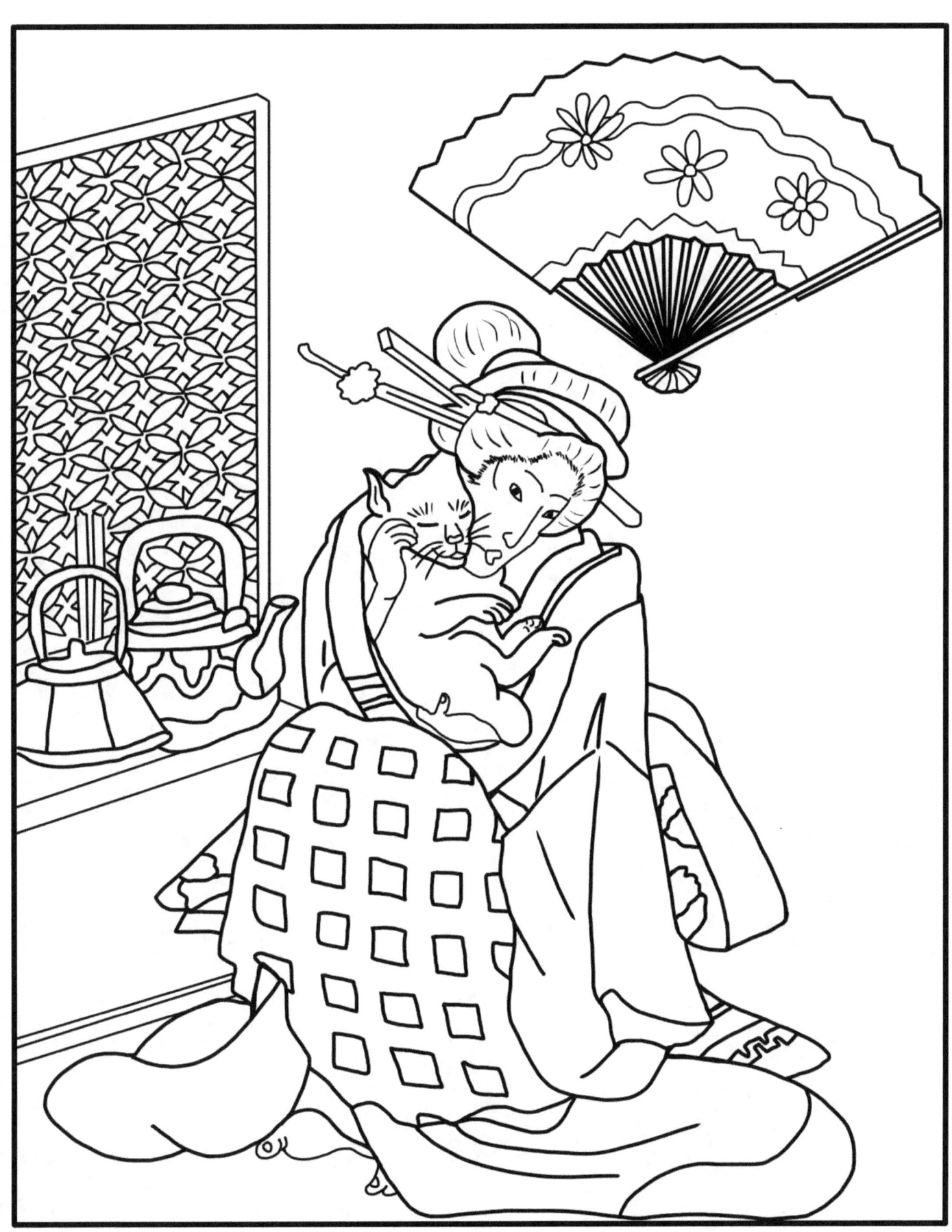

GEISHA AND CAT, KEISAI EISEN

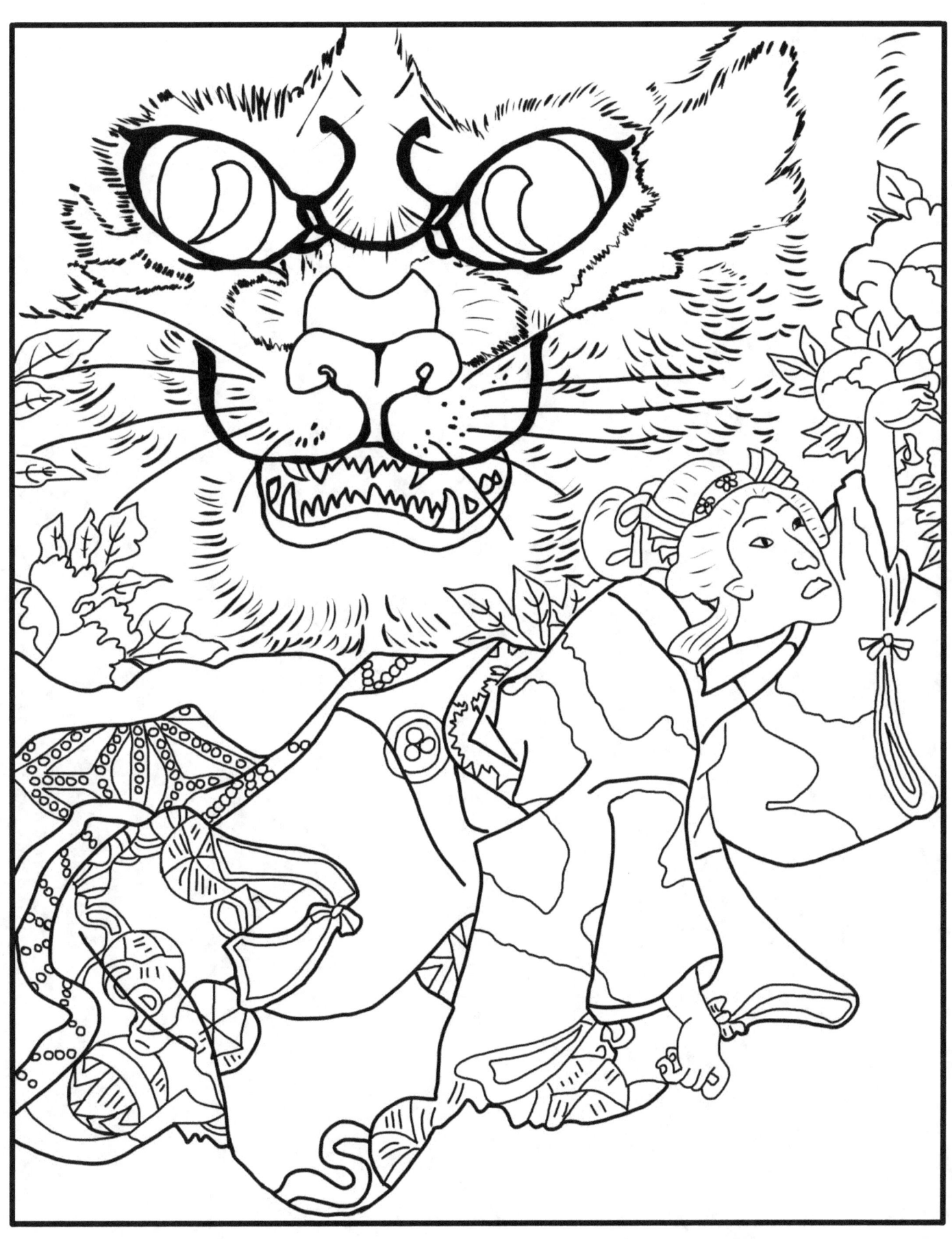

Beloved Concubine Kocho, Utagawa Kunisada, 1853

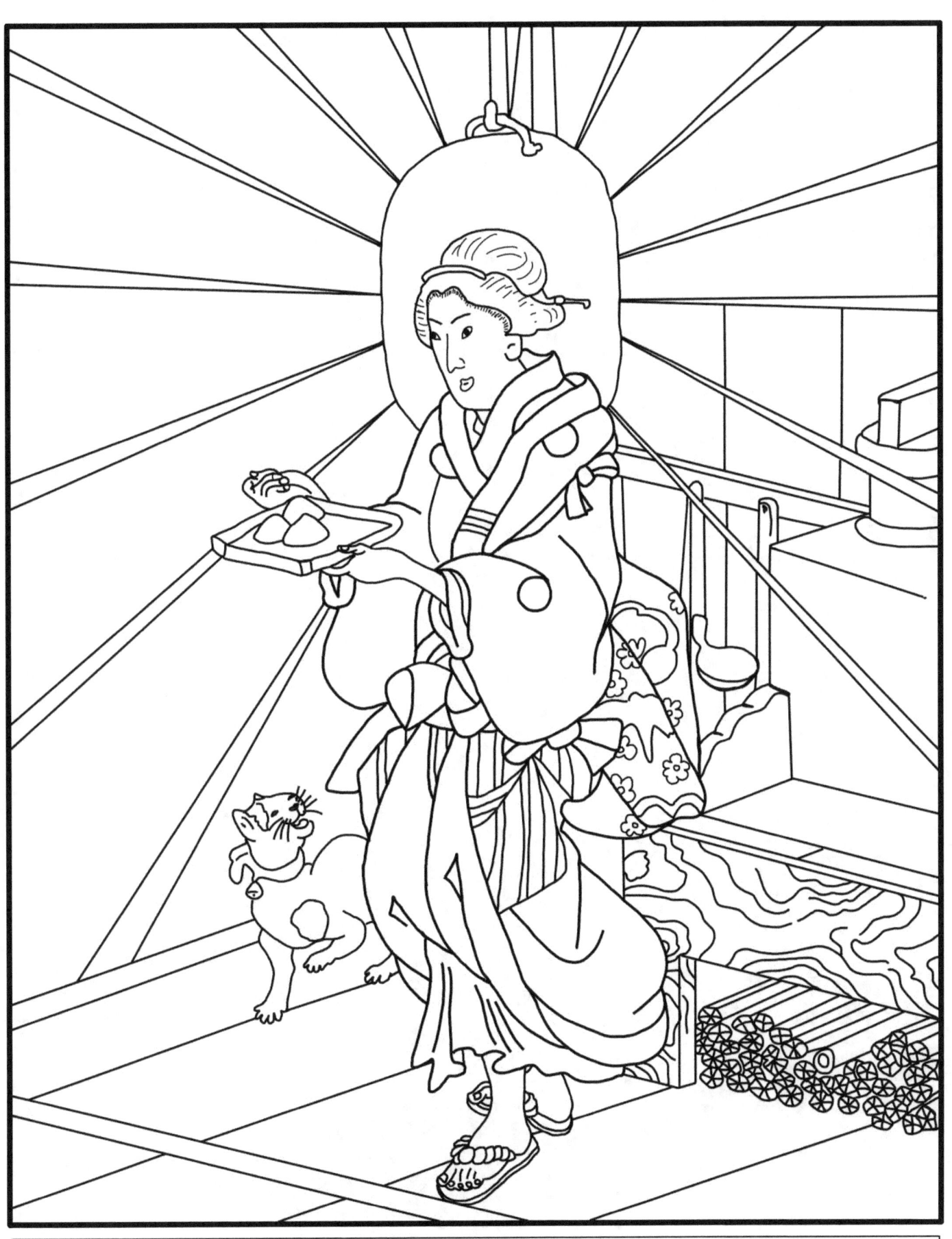

A Brief History of the Buddha Dainichi Disguised as Otake,

Utagawa Kunimaro, 1849

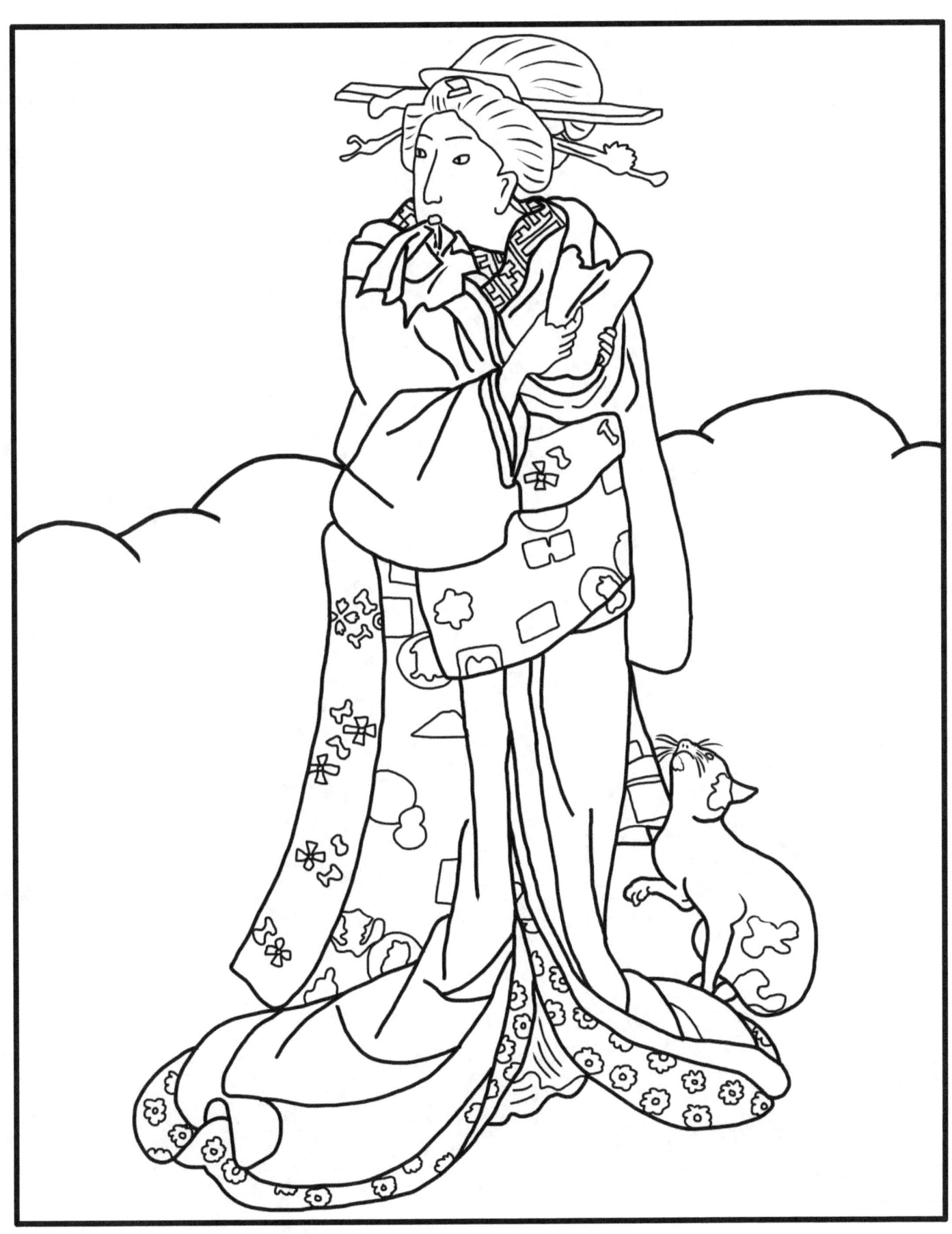

YOUNG LADY AND A CAT, EISEN IKEDA, CA. 1843-1846

ABOUT THE AUTHOR

L.A. Vocelle is an avid cat lover who enjoys pursuing her passion for drawing and writing about cats. She's interested in the role the cat has played in history, art and literature. She has published the following books:

Revered and Reviled: A Complete History of the Domestic Cat

7 Women Artists and their Cat Subjects

Ancient Egyptian Cats: A Coloring Book for Adults and Children

Medieval Cats Coloring Book for Cat Lovers

Cat Breeds Coloring Book 1

Cats and Flowers

L.A. Vocelle posts weekly articles on her website www.thegreatcat.org and continues to be inspired by her five rescue cats.

www.ingramcontent.com/pod-product-compliance
Lightning Source LLC
Chambersburg PA
CBHW080931170526
45158CB00008B/2247